2001

A JOKE ODYSSEY

The Millennium Joke Book

Sandy Ransford has been hooked on humour ever since her first job in publishing – editing the jokes for a well-known magazine – and she has now written more joke books than she can count. Born in South Yorkshire (which may account for it), she now lives in rural mid-Wales surrounded by sheep, with her husband, a horse, a cat, two pygmy goats and two miniature ponies – all of which keep her laughing.

Jane Eccles is a prolific and talented illustrator. She lives in London with her husband, her son Theo, her cat and a great many plants.

Also published by Macmillan

FOOTBALL JOKES
by Sandy Ransford

FOOTBALL PUZZLES
by Sandy Ransford

CUSTARD PIE
Poems that are jokes that are Poems
chosen by Pie Corbett

ALIENS STOLE MY UNDERPANTS
Poems compiled by Brian Moses

DON'T LOOK AT ME IN THAT TONE OF VOICE
Poems by Brian Moses

TONGUE TWISTERS AND TONSIL TWIZZLERS
Poems chosen by Paul Cookson

NOTHING TASTES LIKE A GERBIL
Poems chosen by David Orme

THEY THINK IT'S ALL OVER
Football poems chosen by David Orme

THE KNOCK KNOCK JOKE BOOK
by Sandy Ransford

SPOOKY JOKES
by Sandy Ransford

CHRISTMAS JOKES
by Sandy Ransford

2001

A JOKE ODYSSEY

The Millennium Joke Book

SANDY RANSFORD

Illustrated by
JANE ECCLES

MACMILLAN CHILDREN'S BOOKS

First published 1999 by Macmillan Children's Books
a division of Macmillan Publishers Limited
25 Eccleston Place, London SW1W 9NF
Basingstoke and Oxford
www.macmillan.com

Associated companies throughout the world

ISBN 0 330 34988 0

11 13 15 17 19 18 16 14 12

A CIP catalogue record for this book is available from the British Library.

Typeset in Gill Sans
Printed and bound in Great Britain by Mackays of Chatham plc, Kent.

Contents

Introduction

What better way to celebrate 2,000 years of human history than to have a book crammed with 2,000 jokes? They're all here – doctor jokes, animal jokes, classroom jokes, waiter jokes, knock knocks, elephant jokes, puns, insults, groaners, shaggy dog stories, ghosts, monsters and awful families. Some are as old as time; some brand-new; all, I hope, will make you giggle uncontrollably.

I can't help wondering if anyone wrote a joke book to celebrate the first millennium. This was the time of the Vikings, when Leif Ericson, son of Erik the Red (see page 269) discovered the coast of Nova Scotia. Perhaps a fierce bearded warrior scratched away with a quill pen on a scroll of parchment writing something like this:

YOUNG VIKING: We're going on the ferry to Stavanger tomorrow.
HIS FRIEND: Every time I go on a ferry it makes me cross.

Of course, if the jokes were that bad it could explain why none of these 11th-century joke books survived.

This book will, I hope, do better and survive until the next millennium (i.e. 3000) by which time we'll all be extremely old with white beards so long they'll be tickling our toes! Meanwhile, read on, have fun – and laugh!

In the Beginning

Where could you buy a prehistoric elephant?
At a mammoth sale.

What enormous creature flies into candles on summer nights?
A behemoth.

Which dinosaur ran a cattle ranch in the Wild West?
Tyrannosaurus Tex.

Which dinosaur had to sleep in a soundproof room?
The brontosnaurus.

What did dinosaurs eat for dinner?
Jurassic pork.

What's the difference between a dinosaur and a biscuit?
You can't dip a dinosaur in your tea.

How do dinosaurs pass exams?
With extinction.

Where would you find a prehistoric cow?
In a mooseum.

At what time of the day was Adam born?
Just before Eve.

What didn't Adam and Eve have that everyone else has?
Parents.

Why was Adam the fastest runner in history?
He was first in the human race.

EVE: Do you really love me?
ADAM: Who else?

What did Adam say to Eve that read the same backwards as forwards?
'Madam, I'm Adam.'

Try this rhyme on a friend:

Adam and Eve and Pinch Me went down to the sea to bathe –
Adam and Eve both got drowned, who do you think was saved?

And when your friend replies, 'Pinch Me!' – do so!

What did Adam do when he wanted some sugar?
Raised Cain.

Adam was naming the animals. 'And this,' he said to Eve, 'is a rhinoceros.'

'Why do you call it a rhinoceros?' she asked.

'Because it looks like a rhinoceros, of course,' replied Adam.

What was the first mention of medicine in the Bible?
When God gave Moses the tablets.

How do we know Moses wore a wig?
Because he was sometimes seen with Aaron and sometimes without.

Out of the Ark

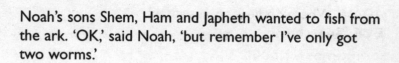

What was Noah's profession?
He was an ark-itect.

What did Noah do when it was dark?
Switched on the floodlights.

Where did Noah keep his bees?
In the ark hives.

Noah's sons Shem, Ham and Japheth wanted to fish from the ark. 'OK,' said Noah, 'but remember I've only got two worms.'

Why didn't the worms go into the ark in an apple?
Because everyone had to go in pairs.

When the Flood had gone down, Noah set all his animals free. Down the gang-plank they walked, as he said, 'Go forth and multiply.' But when they'd all gone he found two snakes sobbing in a corner.
   'Whatever's the matter?' asked Noah.
   'We can't go forth and multiply,' said the snakes sadly. 'You see, we're adders.'

What's green, slimy and goes 'hith'?
A snake with a lisp.

What kind of snakes live on a car?
Vindscreen vipers.

What do you call a fly with no wings?
A walk.

Why did the fly fly?
Because the spider spied 'er.

What do you call a cheerful flea?
A hoptimist.

What happens when a flea gets very angry?
It is hopping mad.

ADAM: Where do fleas go in winter?
EVE: Search me.

FIRST FLEA: You don't look well.
SECOND FLEA: No, I'm not feeling up to scratch.

What bird is always out of breath?
A puffin.

ANNIE: What do birds eat when the bird table's empty?
BILLY: Anything they can find.
ANNIE: What if they can't find anything?
BILLY: They eat something else.

What bird can lift the heaviest weights?
A crane.

What do you call a camel with three humps?
Humphrey.

What does an earwig say when it falls off a wall?
"Ere we go.'

How do you get down from an elephant?
You don't get down from an elephant, you get down from a swan.

How do you stop an elephant going through the eye of a needle?
You tie a knot in his tail.

What's the difference between an African elephant and an Indian elephant?
About 5,000 kilometres.

How did the dragon burn his fingers?
When he yawned he covered his mouth with his hands.

Why did the dragon think himself a failure?
He couldn't give up smoking.

What do hedgehogs like in their cheese sandwiches?
Prickled onions.

What do you call a big goat that picks on little kids?
A bully goat.

What's a goblet?
A little turkey.

What did the river say when the hippo sat in it?
'I'll be dammed.'

What animal with two humps is found at the South Pole?
A lost camel.

Who lost a herd of elephants?
Big Bo Peep.

Why can't you put an elephant in a sandwich?
It's too heavy to lift.

What's the definition of cat?
The one animal that doesn't cry over spilt milk.

Why did the cat join the Red Cross?
It wanted to be a first-aid kit.

What do cats like for breakfast?
Mice krispies.

What do cats read at breakfast?
Mewspapers.

Why does a giraffe have such a long neck?
Because its head is so far from its body.

What did one pig say to another?
'Let's be pen pals.'

Why was the father pig cross with his piglets?
They called him an old boar.

What would happen if pigs could fly?
Bacon would go up.

What do you do with a pig with pimples?
Treat it with oinkment.

What are high-rise pig houses called?
Styscrapers.

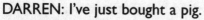

DARREN: I've just bought a pig.
SHARON: Where are you going to keep it?
DARREN: In my wardrobe.
SHARON: But what about the smell?
DARREN: He'll just have to get used to it.

What do you call a stupid pig thief?
A hamburglar.

How can you tell a weasel from a stoat?
A weasel's weasily recognized but a stoat's stoatally different.

HARRY: If you had a black duck and a white duck which would you choose?
LARRY: Eider.

What do you call a bald koala?
Fred Bear.

DILLY: What do you do with a wombat?
MILLY: Play wom, I suppose.

What do you get from nervous cows?
Milk shakes.

What might happen if you walk under a cow?
You might get a pat on the head.

A man was driving along a country lane when his car spluttered to a halt. A cow walked past and said, 'Has it run out of petrol?'

The man was so astonished he went to a nearby farm and told the farmer. 'Was it a Friesian cow – a black and white one?' asked the latter.

The man nodded.

'Then take no notice,' replied the farmer. 'Friesians don't know a thing about cars.'

Whose parrot shouted, 'Pieces of four! Pieces of four!'?
Short John Silver's.

If a whale mother had a son and
a daughter, what would they be called?
Blubber and sister.

Why did the lobster blush?
Because the seaweed.

Why do bees have sticky hair?
Because they use honeycombs.

Why do bees hum?
Because they don't know the words.

What do you call a bee whose buzz you can't quite hear?
A mumble bee.

Where do you take a sick wasp?
To waspital.

Where do wasps come from?
Stingapore.

What do you call two spiders who have just got married?
Newly-webs.

What's the difference between someone who's been
bitten by a mosquito and a bored guest?
One's going to itch; the other's itching to go.

What did the mouse say when it broke its front teeth?
'Hard cheese.'

What do you do if you find a drowning mouse?
Give it mouse to mouse resuscitation.

What's grey, has four legs and a trunk?
A mouse going on holiday.

What's grey, has four legs and two trunks?
A mouse emigrating.

What's the biggest mouse in the world?
A hippopotamouse.

How do you get four elephants in a Mini?
Two in the front and two in the back.

How do you get two whales in a Mini?
Over the Severn Bridge.

Why did the elephant paint her toenails red?
So she could hide in a bowl of cherries.

Why did the elephant dye her hair yellow?
To see if blondes have more fun.

How do you know when there's an elephant in your bed?
By the 'E' on his pyjamas.

How do you know when there's an elephant *under* your bed?
Your head reaches the ceiling.

How do you know when there's an elephant in your fridge?
You can't shut the door.

How can you tell when an elephant has *been* in your fridge?
By the footprints in the butter.

BEN: How big is an elephant?
KEN: What kind of elephant?
BEN: A big one.
KEN: How big?

Why do elephants wear large green hats?
So they can walk across golf courses without being seen.

What did Hannibal say when he saw the elephants crossing the Alps?
'Here come the elephants.'

What did Hannibal say when he saw the elephants crossing the Alps wearing sunglasses?
Nothing, he didn't recognize them.

What's grey and pink, grey and pink, grey and pink?
An elephant with a rose in its trunk rolling down a hill.

What do you give an over-excited elephant?
Trunkquillisers.

What's red on the outside, grey on the inside and very crowded?
A bus full of elephants.

How can you tell when there's an elephant in your custard?
It's very lumpy.

What's the best way to raise an elephant?
Use a fork-lift truck.

Why were the elephants thrown out of the public
swimming baths?
Their trunks fell down

How does an elephant get down from a tree?
He waits until autumn then floats down on a leaf.

Tomb It May Concern

What do you call a friendly Ancient Egyptian?
A chummy mummy.

What do you call an Ancient Egyptian who eats biscuits in bed?
A crumby mummy.

What do you call a mummy who's been eating bread and honey?
A gummy mummy.

Why do mummies make good employees?
They're all wrapped up in their work.

What do they call the puzzle at the top of the Great Pyramid?
A cone-under-'em.

BERTIE: I got told off in school today because I didn't know where the pyramids were.
MUM: I'm always telling you to remember where you put things.

Why was the little Egyptian boy worried?
Because his daddy was a mummy.

Why are mummies good at keeping secrets?
Because they keep everything under wraps.

What do mummies paint on their fingers before going to a party?
Nile varnish.

What did the boy mummy say to the girl mummy?
'Em-balmy about you.'

What did the mummy mummy say as she sent her little girl off to school one winter morning?
'Wrap up well, dear.'

Who does a mummy take to the football match?
Any old pal he can dig up.

Which king of Ancient Egypt was very good at washing dishes?
Pharaoh Liquid.

What do short-sighted mummies wear?
Spooktacles.

How do mummies get out of locked tombs?
They use skeleton keys.

How does a mummy start a letter?
'Tomb it may concern . . .'

What do you call a skeleton that sits around all day?
Lazy bones.

What happened when the skeletons went to the disco?
They had a rattling good time.

What *is* a skeleton?
Bones with people scraped off.

Why didn't the skeleton go to the St Valentine's ball?
Because he had nobody to go with.

What do you call a fat skeleton?
A failure.

Why wouldn't the skeleton go bungee jumping?
He didn't have the guts.

Why did the health-conscious skeleton drink milk?
He'd heard it's good for the bones.

What do you call a royal Scottish skeleton in a kilt?
Bony Prince Charlie.

What did the skeleton say to his friend when they had a row?
'I've a bone to pick with you.'

Why did the skeleton give up his job?
Because his heart wasn't in it.

What's the difference between a skeleton and a supermodel?
Not a lot!

Why was the ghost arrested?
He didn't have a haunting licence.

What jewels do ghosts wear?
Tombstones.

Where does a ghost train stop?
At a manifestation.

What did the teacher ghost say to her pupils?
'Have you got that, boys and girls, or shall we go through it again?'

What do Hungarian ghosts like for supper?
Ghoulash.

What do Italian ghosts like for lunch?
Spookhetti.

What do all ghosts like for breakfast?
Dreaded wheat.

What do you call a drunken ghost?
A methylated spirit.

Where do ghost comedians get their jokes from?
A crypt writer.

What sort of songs do ghosts sing?
Haunting melodies.

Where do ghosts go swimming?
In the Dead Sea.

How does a ghost speak when it's worried?
Gravely.

What do ghosts like on their roast beef?
Gravey.

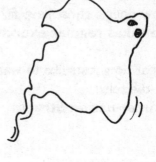

Which ghost made friends with the three bears?
Ghouldilocks.

Where's a good place to spot a ghost?
Lake Erie.

How do ghosts know how high above the ground to float?
They use a spirit level.

FIRST GHOST MOTHER: Hasn't your little ghoul got tall since I last saw her?
SECOND GHOST MOTHER: Yes, she's certainly gruesome.

How do ghosts count?
One, boo, three, four, five, six, seven, hate, nine, frighten!

FIRST GHOST: I'm getting fed up with haunting. We don't seem to frighten people any more.
SECOND GHOST: I know. We might as well be alive for all most of them care.

How does a ghost keep fit?
He takes regular exorcise.

What do ghosts like to watch on the telly?
Horror-nation Street.

Ancient His-tory and Her-story

JIMMY: When did Caesar reign?
TIMMY: I didn't know he rained.
JIMMY: Of course he did. Didn't they hail him?

TEACHER: What was the Romans' greatest achievement?
DIZZY DORA: Being able to speak Latin!

FIRST ROMAN SOLDIER: What's the time?
SECOND ROMAN SOLDIER: XX past VII.

Why did the Romans build straight roads?
So their soldiers didn't go round the bend.

TEACHER: Who can tell me where Hadrian's wall is?
DIM DONALD: I expect it's round Hadrian's garden, Miss.

TEACHER: When was Rome built?
DOPEY DINAH: At night.
TEACHER: Why do you say that?
DOPEY DINAH: Because Dad always says Rome wasn't built in a day.

What did Caesar say to Cleopatra?
'Toga-ether we can rule the world.'

What happened when the slave put his head into the lion's mouth to see how many teeth it had?
The lion closed its mouth to see how many heads the slave had.

Where were the early years of history known as the Dark Ages?
Because there were so many knights.

Why did King Arthur have a round table?
So no one could corner him.

Who invented King Arthur's round table?
Sir Cumference.

What was King Arthur's favourite game?
Knights and crosses.

Why did the knight run up and down at Camelot yelling for a tin opener?
He had a flea in his armour.

What was Camelot?
A place where people parked their camels.

What was Camelot famous for?
Its knight life.

When a knight in armour was killed in battle what sign did they put on his grave?
'Rust in Peace'.

When were King Arthur's army too tired to fight?
When they had lots of sleepless knights.

Knock, knock.
Who's there?
Ivan.
Ivan who?
Not Ivan who, Ivanhoe.

How did the Vikings send secret messages?
By Norse code.

Which English king invented the fireplace?
Alfred the Grate.

Which famous chiropodist ruled England?
William the Corn-curer.

Who invented fractions?
Henry the 1/8.

TEACHER: Whose son was Edward, the Black Prince?
SOPPY SUE: Old King Coal.

Why did Henry VIII have so many wives?
He liked to chop and change.

What was the first thing Queen Elizabeth did on ascending the throne?
Sat down.

What did the ghost of Queen Elizabeth say as it floated into the terrified woman's bedroom?
'Don't be alarmed, madam, I'm just passing through.'

Why was the ghost of Anne Boleyn always running after the ghost of Henry VIII?
She was trying to get ahead.

TEACHER: Where was Magna Carta signed?
SILLY MILLY: At the bottom.

GILLY: I'm learning ancient history.
TILLY: So am I. Let's go for a walk and talk over old times.

Why did Robin Hood only rob the rich?
Because the poor didn't have anything worth stealing.

What did the Sheriff of Nottingham say when Robin
Hood fired him?
'That was an arrow escape.'

What did the dragon say when he met St George, a
knight in shining armour?
'Oh, no, not more tinned food!'

MEDIEVAL LADY: We had roast boar for dinner last
night.
VISITING KNIGHT: Wild?
MEDIEVAL LADY: Well, he wasn't too pleased about it.

A medieval traveller once spent the night at a monastery,
where he was served an excellent meal of fish and chips.
He enjoyed it so much he went into the kitchens to
thank the cook. 'Are you the fish fryer?' he asked.
   'No, I'm the chip monk,' the brother replied.

Christmas Crackers

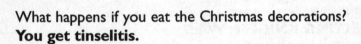

What's Christmas called in England?
Yule Britannia.

What's Santa Claus's wife called?
Mary Christmas.

What happens if you eat the Christmas decorations?
You get tinselitis.

What did one Christmas cracker say to another?
'My pop's bigger than your pop!'

YOUNG MONSTER: Mum, are we having Auntie Betty
for Christmas dinner?
**MOTHER MONSTER: No, dear, I think we'll have
a turkey like most people do.**

What did Santa get when he crossed a reindeer with a
piece of wood?
A hat rack.

Why does Santa go down chimneys?
Because it soots him.

What nationality is Santa Claus?
North Polish.

What exams did Santa take at school?
Ho-ho-ho levels.

What do you call a crate of ducks on 25 December?
A box of Christmas quackers.

Who delivers Christmas presents to cats?
Santa Claws.

What did the bad-tempered man shout out on Christmas Eve?
'I don't care who you are, fat man, get off my roof – and take your animals with you!'

How does Santa begin a joke?
'This one will sleigh you . . .'

What do monkeys sing at Christmas?
'Jungle Bells'.

Mr and Mrs Mousetrouser were on holiday in Moscow, being guided round the sights by a Russian called Rudolf. Just as they were admiring the Kremlin, Mr Mousetrouser looked at the sky and said, 'Look, it's snowing!'

'No,' said Rudolf, 'that's not snow, it's rain.'

'It looks like snow to me,' persisted Mr Mousetrouser.

'Nonsense,' said his wife firmly. 'Rudolf the Red knows rain, dear.'

Why did Harry give Larry a saxophone in a fridge for Christmas?
Because Larry liked to play it cool.

Who used to take Christmas presents to Sherlock Holmes?
Santa Clues.

What happens if you cross a turkey with an octopus?
Everyone can have a leg for Christmas dinner.

SUSIE SPIDER: I don't know what to give my husband for Christmas.
SALLY SPIDER: Do what I did last year – give him four pairs of slippers.

Do you know these alternative carols?

While shepherds washed their socks by night, all seated
    round the tub,
A bar of soap came came rolling down and they began to
    scrub.

Good King Wenceslas looked out
On the Feast of Stephen;
A snowball hit him on the snout –
Made it all uneven.

Brightly shone his conk that night
And the pain was crue-el,
Til a doctor came in sight
Riding on a mu-oo-el.

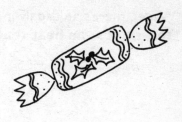

'We three kings of Orient are
Trying to light a rubber cigar.'
It was loaded and exploded –
Blowing them all afar.

Waiter Minute

'Waiter, there's a fly in my soup!'
'Don't worry, sir, the spider on the roll will eat it.'

'Waiter, what's this in my soup?'
'I don't know, sir, all insects look alike to me.'

'Waiter, there's a fly in my soup!'
'Throw him a doughnut, sir, it'll make a good lifebelt.'

'Waiter, there's a dead fly in my soup.'
'Yes, sir, it's the heat that kills them.'

'Waiter, what's this fly doing in my soup?'
'Looks like the breast-stroke, sir.'

'Waiter, there's a fly in my soup!'
'I'm afraid you'll have to get it out yourself, sir, I can't swim.'

'Waiter, there's a fly in my wine!'
'You did ask for something with a little body, sir.'

'Waiter, why is my toast all crumbs?'
'You did ask me to step on it, sir.'

'Waiter, I've found a slug in my lettuce!'
'That's better than finding half a slug, sir.'

'Waiter, this egg's bad!'
'Don't blame me, sir, I only laid the table.'

'Waiter, bring me an elephant sandwich.'
'I'm sorry, sir, we don't do elephant sandwiches.'
'Why not?'
'We haven't enough bread.'

WAITER: And how did you find your cutlet, sir?'
DINER: I just moved a chip and there it was.

'Waiter, is this cottage pie?'
'Yes, sir.'
'Well, fetch a doctor, I think I've just eaten a window.'

'Waiter, there's no chicken in this chicken pie.'
'There aren't any shepherds in the shepherd's pie, either.'

DINER: How much do you charge for dinner?
WAITER: £30 a head, sir.
DINER: In that case, just bring me an ear.

DINER: What kind of soup is this?
WAITER: It's bean soup, sir.
DINER: I don't care what it's been, what is it now?

DINER: My plate's all wet.
WAITER: That's the soup, sir.

DINER: Waiter, why is my mineral water all cloudy?
WAITER: It isn't, sir, it's the glass that's dirty.

'I'll have the steak pie, please.'
'Anything with it, sir?'
'If it's the same as it usually is, a hammer and chisel.'

'Waiter, this pie is terrible. Fetch me the manager!'
'It's no use, sir, he won't eat it, either.'

WAITER: What can I get you, sir?
DINER: A crocodile sandwich, please, and make it snappy.

DINER: I'll have the stale pie, the burnt chips and the watery cabbage.
WAITER: We couldn't possibly serve you food like that, sir.
DINER: Why not? You did yesterday.

DINER: This stew tastes funny.
WAITER: Then why aren't you laughing, sir?

DINER: What's wrong with this fish?
WAITER: Long time no sea, sir.

DINER: Have you minestrone soup on the menu?
WAITER: We did have, but I cleaned it off, sir.

DINER: A glass of milk and a piece of fish, please.
WAITER: Fillet, sir?
DINER: Yes, please, to the top of the glass.

DINER: Waiter, have you smoked salmon?
WAITER: No, sir, I've only ever smoked a pipe.

'Waiter, what's that fly doing on my ice-cream?'
'Looks as if it's learning to ski, sir.'

DINER: Is this coffee or tea?
WAITER: Which did you order, sir?

DINER: Is this coffee or tea? It tastes like paraffin.
WAITER: Then it's tea. The coffee tastes like washing-up water.

DINER: This coffee is very weak.
WAITER: What do you expect me to do, sir, give it weight-training?

WAITER: And what will you have to follow the roast pork, sir?
DINER: Indigestion, I expect.

'Waiter, there's a film on my soup.'
'Sorry, sir, have you seen it before?'

'Waiter, this plate is dirty.'
'It's not my fingerprint, sir.'

'Waiter, this cheese is all soapy.'
'That's to wash your meal down with, sir.'

'Waiter, how long will my sausages be?'
'About 10 cm, sir.'

'Waiter, this food isn't fit for a pig.'
'I'm sorry, sir, I'll bring you some that is.'

DINER: Have you frogs' legs?
WAITER: No, sir, it's just that my shoes are uncomfortable.

DINER: I've been waiting nearly an hour for my turtle soup.
WAITER: I'm sorry, sir, but you know how slow turtles are.

DINER: Why is there a fly in my gravy?
WAITER: I'm sorry, sir, it must have committed insecticide.

DINER: Waiter, will my pizza be long?
WAITER: No, sir, round like everyone else's.

'Waiter, this curry is terrible!'
'Sir, the chef has been making curries since before you were born.'
'Maybe, but why did he have to save one for me?'

'Waiter, this lobster's only got one claw.'
'It must have been in a fight, sir.'
'Then bring me the winner.'

'Waiter, your thumb is in my soup!'
'That's all right, sir, it's not hot.'

'Waiter, there's only one piece of meat on my plate.'
'Sorry, sir, I'll cut it in two.'

Medical Mirth

'Doctor, doctor, I feel like a pair of curtains!'
'Come in and pull yourself together.'

'Doctor, doctor, I feel like a goat!'
'How long has this been going on?'
'Ever since I was a kid.'

'Doctor, doctor, people keep throwing me in the dustbin!'
'Don't talk rubbish.'

'Doctor, doctor, I've only got 30 seconds to live!'
'Sit over there for a minute.'

'Doctor, doctor, can you help me out?''
'Certainly – which way did you come in?'

'Doctor, doctor, I feel like a dog.'
'Sit down over there.'
'I can't, I'm not allowed on the chairs.'

'Doctor, doctor, my brother thinks he's a hen.'
'Why don't you take him to a psychiatrist?'
'Because we need the eggs.'

'Doctor, doctor, my brother thinks he's a lift.'
'Tell him to come in to the surgery.'
'He can't, he doesn't stop at this floor.'

'Doctor, doctor, I feel like a racehorse!'
'Take these pills every two furlongs.'

'Doctor, doctor, I feel like a bee!'
'Buzz off, will you?'

'Doctor, doctor, I think I'm shrinking!'
'You'll just have to be a little patient.'

'Doctor, doctor, I've just swallowed a roll of film!'
'Let's hope nothing develops.'

'Doctor, doctor, I keep thinking I'm a sheep!'
'How do you feel?'
'Very baaaad.'

'Doctor, doctor, I keep shoplifting!'
'Have you taken anything for it?'

'Doctor, doctor, I keep seeing double!'
'Sit on that chair, please.'
'Which one?'

'Doctor, doctor, I've swallowed a spoon!'
'Lie down and don't stir.'

'Doctor, doctor, I think I'm a £5 note!'
'Go shopping, you need the change.'

'Doctor, doctor, people keep telling me I'm a cricket bat!'
'Howzat?'
'Oh, not you too!'

'Doctor, doctor, I feel like a guitar!'
'Sit down while I make some notes.'

'Doctor, doctor, I can't sleep!'
'Lie on the edge of the bed, you'll soon drop off.'

'Doctor, doctor, will this ointment make my skin better?'
'I never make rash promises.'

'Doctor, doctor, I think I'm a doorknob!'
'Don't fly off the handle.'

'Doctor, doctor, I feel like an old sock!'
'Well, I'll be darned!'

'Doctor, doctor, I feel like a bridge!'
'What's come over you today?'

'Doctor, doctor, can you give me something for my liver?'
'How about a pound of onions?'

'Doctor, doctor, I feel like a damson.'
'You are in a jam, aren't you?'

'Doctor, doctor, I feel like a canary!'
'Perch over there and I'll tweet you in a minute.'

'Doctor, doctor, I'm a compulsive liar.'
'I don't believe you.'

'Doctor, doctor, I think I'm invisible!'
'Next, please!'

'Doctor, doctor, I feel like a yo-yo.'
'Sit down, sit down, sit down.'

How do you cure water on the brain?
With a tap on the head.

DOCTOR: Take one of these pills three times a day.
PATIENT: How can I take it more than once?

PATIENT: I snore so loudly I keep myself awake. What can I do?
DOCTOR: Sleep in another room.

DOCTOR: Is your cough better this morning?
PATIENT: It should be, I've been practising all night.

DOCTOR: How are you today?
PATIENT: I'm still having trouble breathing, doctor.
DOCTOR: I'll give you something to stop that.

PATIENT: Is it serious, doctor?
DOCTOR: Put it this way, don't start watching any TV serials.

PATIENT: Can you give me something for flat feet?
DOCTOR: How about a bicycle pump?

PATIENT: Will the pills you've given me make me better?
DOCTOR: No one I've given them to has ever been back.

DOCTOR: Are those pills I gave you to improve your memory working?
PATIENT: What pills?

DOCTOR: How did you get that splinter in your finger?
PATIENT: I scratched my head.

PATIENT: I feel half dead.
DOCTOR: I'll arrange for you to be buried up to your middle.

PATIENT: Can you give me something for wind?
DOCTOR: Certainly, here's a kite.

DOCTOR: Stand over by the window and put out your tongue, please.
PATIENT: Is that so you can see it in the daylight?
DOCTOR: No, I just dislike the people across the road.

DOCTOR: Breathe out deeply, please.
PATIENT: Do you want to check my lungs?
DOCTOR: No, I want to clean my glasses.

PATIENT: How do I stand, doctor?
DOCTOR: I've no idea, it must be a miracle.

PATIENT: Can you help me? I'm at death's door.
DOCTOR: Don't worry, I'll soon pull you through.

PATIENT: There's something wrong with my stomach.
DOCTOR: Keep your coat buttoned up and no one will notice.

PATIENT: Those pills you gave me to improve my strength aren't doing me any good at all.
DOCTOR: Why not?
PATIENT: I can't unscrew the bottle.

PATIENT: I swallowed a clock last month.
DOCTOR: This could be serious. Why didn't you come and see me sooner?
PATIENT: I didn't want to alarm you.

PATIENT: I'm very nervous, you see, it's the first operation I've ever had.
DOCTOR: I know how you feel – it's the first I've ever performed.

PATIENT: I can't sleep a wink most nights.
DOCTOR: Have you tried counting sheep?
PATIENT: Yes. But I got up to 3,848,932 and it was time to get up.

PATIENT: My husband thinks he's a door.
DOCTOR: Call me when he's unhinged.

PATIENT: My husband thinks he's a squirrel.
DOCTOR: He must be a nut case.

'Doctor, doctor, do you think I need glasses?'
'You certainly do, this is the post office.'

DOCTOR: Say 'one hundred' please.
PATIENT: Why not 'ninety-nine'?
DOCTOR: Inflation, you know.

DOCTOR: You should have sent for me sooner. Your wife is seriously ill.
MR WOBBLETUM: I thought I'd give her a chance to get better first.

'Doctor, doctor, I feel run down. What should I take?'
'The number of the car that hit you.'

Cross Purposes

What do you get if you cross a chicken with a dog?
Pooched eggs.

What do you get if you cross a complaining man with a spacecraft?
A moan rocket.

What do you get if you cross an elephant with a budgie?
A bird with a very dirty cage.

What do you get if you cross an elephant with a spider?
I don't know, but if it crawls across your ceiling you'd better watch out!

What do you get if you cross an elephant with a goose?
An animal that honks before it knocks you down.

What do you get if you cross an elephant with an insect?
A forget-me-gnat.

What do you get if you cross a cow with a carpet?
A thick pile all over the floor.

What do you get if you cross a birthday cake with a tin of baked beans?
A cake that blows out its own candles.

What do you get if you cross a terrier with a vegetable?
A Jack Brussel.

What do you get if you cross a gundog with a phone?
A golden receiver.

What do you get if you cross a sheepdog with a vegetable?
A collie flower.

What do you get if you cross a cocoa bean with an elk?
A chocolate moose.

What do you get if you cross King Kong with a bell?
A ding-dong King Kong.

What do you get if you cross a rabbit with a leek?
A bunion.

What do you get if you cross the Atlantic with the *Titanic*?
Halfway.

What do you get if you cross a tractor with a dog?
A Land Rover.

What do you get if you cross a dog with a cat?
An animal that chases itself.

What do you get if you cross an elephant with a computer?
A great big know-all.

What do you get if you cross a cow with a shelled super-hero?
A moo-tant ninja turtle.

What do you get if you cross a tremor with a duck?
An earthquack.

What do you get if you cross a book with an acrobat?
A book that can turn its own pages.

What do you get if you cross a centipede with an elephant?
A creature that trips over its nose 100 times.

What do you get if you cross a camera with a dentist?
A man with a film on his teeth.

What do you get if you cross a journalist with a hunting-dog?
A newshound.

What do you get if you cross a hamburger with a novel?
A fast food store-y.

What do you get if you cross a choir boy with a plate of mince?
A hymn-burger.

What do you get if you cross a jelly with a sheepdog?
Collie-wobbles.

What do you get if you cross a kangaroo with a sheep?
A woolly jumper with pockets.

What do you get if you cross a chicken with a bell?
An alarm cluck.

What do you get if you cross a chef with a rooster?
A cook-a-doodle-do.

What do you get if you cross a chicken with a load of cement?
A brick-layer.

What do you get if you cross a chicken with an elephant?
Enough feathers to stuff a duvet.

What do you get if you cross a herd of cows with a flock of ducks?
Milk and quackers.

What do you get if you cross an elephant with a cockerel?
A creature that wakes up people in the next county.

What do you get if you cross an elephant with a mouse?
Huge holes in the skirting-board!

What do you get if you cross an elephant with a cat?
Very nervous mice.

What do you get if you cross an elephant with a squirrel?
An animal that remembers where it stored its nuts.

What do you get if you cross an elephant with an apple?
A pie that never forgets.

What do you get if you cross a sheep with an octopus?
A sweater with eight sleeves.

What do you get if you cross a sheep with a grasshopper?
A woolly jumper.

What do you get if you cross a sheep with a thunderstorm?
A wet blanket.

What do you get if you cross an alley cat with a canary?
A peeping tom.

What do you get if you cross an ant-hill with a window-box?
Ants in your plants.

What do you get if you cross a bee with a slice of beef?
A humburger.

What do you get if you cross a wimp and a sweet on a stick?
A wallypop.

What do you get if you cross a lion with a parrot?
I don't know, but when it says 'Pretty Polly' you should smile.

Classroom Capers

TEACHER: What's your father's name?
SMALL BOY AT FIRST SCHOOL: The same as mine, Evans.
TEACHER: No, I mean his first name.
SMALL BOY: I don't know.
TEACHER: Well, what name does your mother call him?
SMALL BOY: She doesn't call him names, she likes him.

TEACHER: If you had £2.50 in one pocket and £3.78 in the other, what would you have?
LITTLE JAMIE: Someone else's trousers.

TEACHER: Spell 'horse'.
JENNY: H, o, r, s.
TEACHER: Yes, but what's on the end of it?
JENNY: A tail.

TEACHER: What in the alphabet comes after O?
SILLY BILLY: Yeah.

DAD: How were the exam questions?
DAVE: Fine. It was the answers I had trouble with.

ANNIE: How old do you think our teacher is?
DANNY: I don't know, but I've heard his grandfather was called Adam.

TEACHER: Why don't you write more clearly?
LUCY: Because then you'd realize I can't spell.

TEACHER: Why were you late for school?
SALLY: I had to say goodbye to my pets.
TEACHER: But you're two hours late!
SALLY: I keep bees.

TEACHER: If you had to divide 2,345 by 7 what would you get?
GEORGE: The wrong answer.

TEACHER: When were you born?
DARREN: Why, do you want to give me a birthday present?

TEACHER: If your father earned £750 a week and gave your mother half, what would she have?
DANIEL: Heart failure.

TEACHER: Don't whistle while you're studying.
CHARLIE: I'm not studying, just whistling.

HARRY: My brother's teachers say he will soon get ahead.
LARRY: That's good, because he looks funny with nothing on top of his neck.

TEACHER: And what might your name be, little boy?
NAUGHTY PUPIL: It might be Liam Gallagher, but it isn't.

Why is an old car like a classroom?
Because it has a lot of nuts and a crank up front.

Young William came home from school one day groaning and holding his stomach. 'Are you in pain?' asked his anxious mum.
'No,' said William, 'the pain's in me.'

BOBBY: I've got to write an essay on an elephant.
NOBBY: You'll need a ladder.

BRIAN: Your teacher has such a sympathetic face.
RYAN: How do you mean?
BRIAN: Whenever I see her I feel sympathy for her.

MATHS TEACHER: If I had ten apples in one hand and 12 in the other, what would I have?
CLASS: The biggest hands anyone's ever seen.

MARY: Do you know a boy called Clarence?
CARY: Yes, he sleeps next to me in history.

BEN: I've got a part in the school Christmas play.
KEN: What part?
BEN: I'm one of the three wise guys.

TEACHER: That essay you wrote on 'My Dog' is exactly the same as your sister's.
JANICE: I know. It's the same dog.

DENNIS: Remember you promised me £10 if I passed my maths exam?
DAD: Yes.
DENNIS: Well, I have good news for you, I've just saved you £10.

TEACHER: Who can tell me what 5 x 5 is?
LAURA: Twenty-five.
TEACHER: Good.
LAURA: Good? It was perfect!

NORA: I've added these figures up ten times.
TEACHER: Good.
NORA: And here are my ten answers.

What did one maths textbook say to the other?
'Boy, have I got problems!'

LITTLE JIMMY: I can't find my boots.
**TEACHER: Are you sure these aren't yours?
They're the only ones left.**
LITTLE JIMMY: Quite sure. Mine were covered in snow.

Milly's English teacher went to Milly's house and asked to see Milly's mum.
  'She ain't in,' said Milly.
  'Milly!' cried her teacher, 'where's your grammar?'
  'She ain't in neither,' replied Milly.

BOY ON PHONE: I'm afraid Graham can't come to school today because he has a cold.
TEACHER: To whom am I speaking?
BOY ON PHONE: This is my father.

Pam and Sam were talking about school dinners. 'I think it's UFOs again today,' said Pam.
   'What's that?' asked Sam.
   'Unidentified Frying Objects.'

What's the difference between school tapioca pudding and frogspawn?
Not a lot.

DAVE: Yesterday we had Enthusiasm Stew for dinner.
MAVE: What's that?
DAVE: It's when the cook puts everything she's got into it.

TEACHER: Can anyone tell me the longest word in the dictionary?
RANI: 'Elastic', Miss.
TEACHER: It can't be, it's only got seven letters.
RANI: Yes, Miss, but it stretches.

TEACHER: Did you know Columbus found America?
ELLA: I didn't even know it was lost.

Which class in school does Coca-Cola like best?
Phys. Ed.

TRACEY: Why are you going to night school?
STACEY: I want to learn to do sums in the dark.

NED: Did you get a good place in the maths test?
TED: I'll say. I sat next to the brainiest kid in the class.

TEACHER: I hope I didn't see you copying, Samantha.
SAMANTHA: I hope you didn't either, Miss.

TEACHER: What did Caesar say when Brutus stabbed him?
ABDUL: 'Ouch!'

What does an idiot study when he has a chemistry exam the following day?
His geography notes.

TEACHER: And how do you handle temptation, young Nicky?
NICKY: I yield to it.

TEACHER: What's a prickly pear?
VICKY: Two hedgehogs.

TEACHER: Who can tell me what the guillotine was?
SMART ALEC: A pain in the neck.

TEACHER: What's half of 8?
JERRY: Up and down or across?
TEACHER: What do you mean?
JERRY: Well, up and down it's 3, but across it's 0.

TEACHER: What would you say if I came to school with a face as dirty as yours, Daniel?
DANIEL: I'd be too polite to mention it.

TEACHER: I told you to write this extract out ten times to try and improve your handwriting, but you've only done it four times. Why's that?
ANDY: My maths is bad, too.

'If two's company and three's a crowd what's four and five?'
'Don't know.'
'Nine.'

If buttercups are yellow, what colour are hiccups?
Burple.

Why is history like a fruit cake?
It's full of dates.

Why wasn't Dave any good at history?
He believed in letting bygones be bygones.

Who were the Incas?
The first people to write with fountain pens.

JENNY: Mum, will you do my homework for me?
MUM: No, Jenny, it wouldn't be right.
JENNY: It won't be right if I do it either.

TEACHER: Which is further away from Britain, the moon or Australia?
KEVIN: Australia.
TEACHER: Why do you say that?
KEVIN: Because you can see the moon but you can't see Australia.

TEACHER: What's the plural of 'baby'?
LYN: Twins?

TEACHER: Who was Ivanhoe?
GLYN: A Russian gardener.

UNCLE: And do you like Kipling, my boy?
JOHNNY: I don't know, I've never kippled.

TEACHER: You look rather pale this morning, Andrew, are you all right?
ANDREW: Oh yes, Miss. I must have overwashed.

TEACHER: What are you drawing?
JILL: A pony eating grass.
TEACHER: Where's the grass?
JILL: The pony ate it all.
TEACHER: And where's the pony?
JILL: He went home, he didn't want to stay in a field with no grass in it.

TEACHER: And what are you drawing, Carol?
CAROL: A picture of heaven.
TEACHER: But no one knows what heaven looks like.
CAROL: But they will when I've finished, won't they?

TEACHER: Hands up all those who want to go to heaven. Why isn't your hand up, Jimmy? Don't you want to go to heaven?
JIMMY: Oh yes, Miss, but Mum says I must go straight home after school.

SILLY WILLY: Our school's haunted.
DAD: What makes you think that?
SILLY WILLY: The headmaster's always talking about the
school spirit.

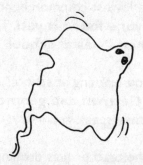

TEACHER: Can you tell me what nationality Napoleon
was, Timmy?
REST OF CLASS: Corsican!

What did the paper say to the pencil?
'Write on!'

What did the pencil say to the eraser?
'Take me to your ruler.'

Why was the pencil feeling miserable?
It had a leadache.

What's a motel?
William Tell's sister.

Why was the boy late for school?
**He was dreaming about a football match and they
went into extra time.**

TEACHER: Why are you *always* late for school?
BILLY: You always ring the bell before I get here.

MIKE: Dad, will you help me with my homework, please? I'm looking for the lowest common denominator.
DAD: Hasn't anyone found it yet? They were looking for it when I was at school.

DAD: What are you learning at school?
SPIKE: French, German and geometry.
DAD: Where do they speak geometry?

One day in class the teacher was droning on and on when he spotted young Steve had his head under the desk lid. 'What are you doing?' asked the teacher. 'Are you learning something?'

'No, sir,' replied Steve, 'I'm listening to you.'

ENGLISH TEACHER: Did you write this poem, Harry?
HARRY: Yes, Miss.
TEACHER: Pleased to meet you, Lord Tennyson.

Does an apple a day keep a teacher away?
It does if your aim is accurate enough.

TEACHER: Name six things that contain milk.
SUSIE: Ice-cream, custard and four cows.

SCIENCE TEACHER: What happened when electricity was discovered?
MANDY: Someone got a nasty shock.

What's black when clean and white when dirty?
A blackboard.

Why should a school not be near a chicken farm?
So the pupils can't hear fowl language.

TEACHER: Name three collective nouns.
TILLY: The dustbin, the wastepaper basket and the vacuum cleaner.

'Mother, I really don't want to go to school today. Please don't make me.'
'But Harold, you must go. You're the headmaster!'

TEACHER: Who was the first woman in the world?
DINAH: Don't know, Miss.
TEACHER: Yes you do. Remember the story of the apple?
DINAH: Er, Granny Smith, Miss?

Sammy Smith is dead,
We'll never see him more,
For what he thought was H_2O*
Was H_2SO_4.**

* *Water.*
** *Sulphuric acid.*

TEACHER: Why are you crossing the road at this dangerous crossroads? Can't you see there's a zebra crossing 50 metres away?
DAVY: Well I hope it's having better luck than I am.

MUSIC STUDENT: Did you really learn to play the piano in six easy lessons?
MUSIC TEACHER: Yes. It was the 200 that followed that were really difficult.

TEACHER: When you yawn you should put your hand in front of your mouth.
ALAN: What! And get it bitten!

TEACHER: What is the equator?
SILLY BILLY: An imaginary lion running round the world.

TEACHER: What's your name, boy?
BASIL: Basil.
TEACHER: Say 'sir' when you speak to me.
BASIL: All right, Sir Basil.

MOTHER: Do you think William should take up the piano as a career?
TEACHER: No, I think he should put down the lid as a favour.

MARY: Are slugs good to eat, Miss?
TEACHER: Stop asking disgusting questions, Mary and get on with your lunch.
TEACHER, LATER: Now, what was it you were asking, Mary?
MARY: It was about slugs, Miss, but it's too late now. You had one on your plate, but it's gone now.

Did you hear about the cross-eyed teacher?
She couldn't control her pupils.

Layabout Len was sprawling at his desk with his feet stuck out in the aisle, eating chewing-gum.
    'Len!' yelled his teacher. 'Take out that chewing-gum and put your feet in this instant!'

FRENCH TEACHER: What does *moi aussi* mean?
DAFT DAVE: 'I am an Australian.'

TEACHER: How old do you think I am?
JERRY: Thirty-six, sir.
TEACHER: What makes you so sure?
JERRY: Because my big brother's 18 and you're twice as stupid as he is!

JENNY: What did the teacher say about your essay?
KENNY: She took it like a lamb.
JENNY: Really? What did she say?
KENNY: Baaa!

TEACHER: Can you spell 'Mississippi'?
SUSIE: Well, I can start but I'm not sure if I can finish!

How does a teacher keep her class on its toes?
She puts drawing-pins on their chairs!

BARRY: What are the meals like at your school?
LARRY: Put it this way, even the dustbins have indigestion!

COOKERY TEACHER: Who can tell me the secret of making our cakes light?
SALLY: Er, pour petrol on them?

Loony Library

Have you read the following books from the school library?

Seaside Treats by Rhoda Donkey
Pot Plants by Polly Anthus
The Big Bang by Dinah Mite
Droopy Drawers by Lucy Lastic
Taming Wild Cats by Claud Face
The Garlic Eater by I. Malone
Modern Haircuts by Sean Head
Shipwreck! by Mandy Lifeboats
Easy Suppers by Egon Chips
Old English Churches by Beverley Minster
Igloo Building by S. Keemo
Smashing Windows by Eva Stone
Parachute Jumping by Hugo Furst
The Hurricane by Rufus Blownoff
Fitting Carpets by Walter Wall
Collecting Litter by Phil D. Basket
Mega Bites by Amos Quito
Vegetable Gardening by Rosa Cabbages
Improve Your Gardening by Anita Lawn
Continental Breakfasts by Roland Butter
Weekend Breaks by Gladys Friday
Keep On Trying by Percy Vere
Cheese and Salami by Della Katessen
Country Dancing by Hans Kneesanboomsadaisy
Catching Criminals by Hans Upp
Whodunnit? by Ivor Clew

Throwing a Party by Maud D. Merrier
Winning the Lottery by Jack Potts
The Runaway Horse by Gay Topen
A Knock on the Head by Esau Starrs
How to Make Money by Robin Banks
Your Money or Your Life by Stan Den Deliver
Seasons' Greetings by Mary Christmas
My Life as an Estate Agent by Con Allday
Adding Up by Juan and Juan
Easter Eggs by Ken I. Havesum
Telecommunications by Ron Number
Packed Lunches by Sam Widge
Aching Joints by Arthur Itis
Birdwatching by Jack Daw
My Life in the Police Force by Iris Tew

Do You Love Me?

SHE: Do you really love me?
HE: **Of course.**
SHE: Then whisper something soft and sweet in my ear.
HE: **Lemon meringue pie.**

GLORIA: I wish I had a penny for every boy who's asked me out.
GLADYS: **Then you'd be able to afford to use a public lavatory.**

DEAN: What would it take to get you to kiss me?
JEAN: **An anaesthetic.**

TIM: Why is your face all scratched?
JIM: **My girlfriend said it with flowers.**
TIM: How romantic.
JIM: **Not really. She hit me round the face with a bunch of thorny roses.**

JACK: I'm not rich like Albert, and I don't have a mansion like Brian or an Aston Martin like Cecil, but I love you and I want to marry you.
JILL: **I love you too, but what did you say about Cecil?**

ROMEO: Do you like me?
JULIET: **As boys go, you're OK, and the further you go the better.**

'Your teeth are like the stars,' he said,
As he pressed her hand so white.
He spoke the truth, for, like the stars,
Her teeth came out at night.

MRS BROWN: Where are you off to?
MRS GREEN: The doctor's. I don't like the look of my husband.
MRS BROWN: Can I come with you? I can't stand the sight of mine!

DARREN: Could you be happy with a boy like me?
SHARON: Maybe, if you weren't around too often.

VIC: She's such a nice bird.
NICK: She must be if she goes out with a worm like you.

FREDDIE: The computer dating agency picked me out as the ideal boyfriend.
EDDIE: But who wants to go out with a computer?

TRACEY: My boyfriend says I'm beautiful.
STACEY: They do say love is blind.

MRS BLACK: My husband's a man of many parts.
**MRS WHITE: Pity they weren't put together
properly.**

'What happened to that couple who met in a revolving
door?'
'They're still going around together.'

SUITOR: I've come to ask for your daughter's hand.
**FATHER: You'll have to take the rest of her too
or the deal's off.**

JAKE: Girls whisper they love me.
**BLAKE: Well, they'd hardly say it out loud, would
they?**

'My brother fell in love with his wife the second time he
saw her. The first time he didn't know how rich she was.'

'She wears her engagement ring on the wrong finger.'
**'She probably feels she's engaged to the wrong
man.'**

BILL: What did you buy your girlfriend for Christmas?
WILL: A bottle of toilet water. It cost me £15.
BILL: If you'd come to our house you could have had as
much water as you wanted out of our toilet for free.

'He has a leaning towards redheads.'
'Yes, but they keep pushing him back.'

'She was two-thirds married once.'
'What do you mean?'
'She turned up, the minister turned up, but the groom didn't.'

'Why do they call her an after-dinner speaker?'
'Because every time she speaks to a man she's after a dinner.'

SALLY: Did he really marry her because her grandfather left her a fortune?
CALLY: He denies it. He says he'd have married her no matter who had left her a fortune.

PATTIE: His girlfriend returned all his letters.
MATTIE: I bet she marked them 'second-class male'.

JENNY: I wish you were on TV.
KENNY: Would you love me if I were a TV star?
JENNY: No, but I could switch you off.

MANDY: My boyfriend's really clever. He has brains enough for two.
SANDY: He sounds like the right boy for you.

CUTHBERT: I can't leave you.
CLARICE: Do you love me that much?
CUTHBERT: It's not that, you're standing on my foot.

LARRY: I got a lovely Persian kitten for my girlfriend.
HARRY: I wish I could make a trade like that.

'My sister wanted to marry a man clever enough to make a lot of money and dumb enough to spend it on her.'

'I wouldn't say your girlfriend has a big mouth but when she yawns her ears vanish.'

KATE: When I grow up I'm going to marry the boy next door.
CLARE: Why?
KATE: I'm not allowed to cross the road.

MR WHITE: Why do you want to be buried at sea?
MR BLACK: To stop my wife from dancing on my grave.

What do cannibals do at a wedding?
Toast the bride and groom.

JOE: What happened to that dumb blonde I used to go out with?
MO: I dyed my hair.

SHARON: Now we're engaged I hope you'll give me a ring.
DARREN: Of course. What's your phone number?

LADY IN SHOP TO JEWELLER: If my husband doesn't like this diamond necklace will you refuse to take it back?

RONALD: My brother's girlfriend has beautiful long blonde hair all down her back.
DONALD: What a pity it's not on her head.

WAYNE: I can marry anyone I please.
JAYNE: But you don't please anyone.

BOSS: Why do you want time off next week?
CLERK: To get married.
BOSS: What stupid woman would marry you?
CLERK: Your daughter.

If Miss Piggy married Mr Back she'd be Piggy Back.

JACK: Have you noticed how many girls don't want to get married nowadays?
JAKE: No. How do you know?
JACK: I've asked them all.

MILES: The girl I marry will have to be able to take a joke.
GILES: That's the only kind you'll get.

GERRY: Why aren't you going to marry Jack after all?
KERRY: He said he'd die if I didn't, so I thought I'd wait and see . . .

FATHER: It's time you found a wife and left home, Marmaduke. When I was your age I'd been married for years.
MARMADUKE: But you were married to Mum. You wouldn't want me to marry a stranger, would you?

SUITOR: Sir, I'd like your daughter for my wife.
FATHER: Can't she get one of her own?

JAN: Boys fall in love with me at first sight.
ANNE: Yes, but at the second and third sights they realize they can't stand you!

'Before she was married your sister turned her husband's head with her good looks. Now she turns his stomach with her cooking.'

SOLLY: Last night I dreamt I was dancing with the most beautiful girl in the world.
POLLY: What was I wearing?

GEORGE: I'll cook you dinner. What would you like?
GEORGINA: A life insurance policy.

TINA: Annie's boyfriend told her he'd lost all his money.
GINA: What did she say?
TINA: 'I'll miss you, darling.'

They're perfectly matched. He's blinded by love and her looks are out of sight.

They're perfectly matched. He's a history teacher and she likes dates.

They're perfectly matched. She likes jogging and he was on the run from the law.

They're perfectly matched. She works in a chip shop and there's something fishy about him.

They're perfectly matched. She's a geologist and he's on the rocks.

When Plus and Minus got married they had an addition to the family. Trouble is, he turned out to be a problem child.

MR GREEN: My wife's one in a million.
MR BROWN: Really? I thought she was won in a raffle.

What's the wife of a hippie called?
Mississippi.

MRS SMITH: Don't you think that man over there is the ugliest person you've ever seen?
MRS JONES: He's my husband.
MRS SMITH: Oh dear, I'm so sorry.
MRS JONES: You're sorry . . .

MR DIM: Here, you just shot my wife.
MR DUMB: I'm so sorry – have a shot at mine.

GILLIE: Have you had any replies to your advert for a husband?
TILLY: Yes, and they all say the same thing.
GILLIE: What's that?
TILLY: 'You can have mine.'

A woman woke her husband one night and said, 'There's a burglar in the kitchen eating my home-made steak and kidney pie!'
'Oh dear,' said her husband. 'Who shall I call, police or ambulance?'

MARTHA: If you were my husband I'd put arsenic in your tea.
ARTHUR: And if I were your husband I'd drink it.

Which group of men on TV wear pastel-coloured suits and can't speak properly?
The telehubbies.

JULIET: You remind me of the sea.
ROMEO: Because I'm wild, unpredictable and romantic?
JULIET: No, because you make me sick.

GLYN: You must marry me, or I'll blow my brains out.
LYN: Go ahead, you've nothing to lose.

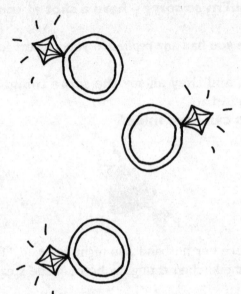

On the Move

BILLY: How fast does light travel?
MILLY: I don't know, but it always arrives too early in the morning.

NERVOUS PASSENGER ON PLANE: How often do planes like this crash?
STEWARDESS: Only once, sir.

NERVOUS PASSENGER ON SHIP: How far are we from land?
STEWARD: About four kilometres, sir.
NERVOUS PASSENGER: In which direction?
STEWARD: Downwards!

MAN ON PHONE: How long does it take to fly to Hong Kong?
TRAVEL AGENT: Just a minute, sir . . .
MAN ON PHONE: Thanks very much.

DAVE: In Australia people chase kangaroos on horseback.
MAVE: Fancy that! I didn't know kangaroos could ride horses!

What happens if you dial 666 in Australia?
A policeman comes along walking on his hands.

Why do Eskimos eat whalemeat and blubber?
Wouldn't you blubber if you had to eat whalemeat?

Which country has no fat people?
Finland.

Who waves a magic wand and goes from Dover to Calais?
A cross-Channel fairy.

What's tall and wet and stands in the middle of Paris?
The Eiffel Shower.

Why is honey scarce in Bermuda?
There's only one B in Bermuda.

MRS TRELLIS: So you're not going to Spain for your holidays this year?
MRS ELLIS: No, that was last year. This year we're not going to Italy.

JENNY: How do you top a car?
BENNY: Tep on the brake, tupid.

CUTHBERT: Hello, old top! New car?
CLARENCE: No, old car. New top.

CROSS CAR BUYER: You said this was a good car, but it won't go up hills.
SECONDHAND CAR DEALER: On the level, it's a good car.

Why can't a car play football?
Because it's only got one boot.

Did you hear about the bike that went round and round biting people?

It was known as the vicious cycle.

Janet and John were riding a tandem up a hill and finding it very hard work.

'Phew!' said Janet at the top. 'I never thought we'd make it!'

'Nor did I,' replied John. 'It's a good thing I kept the brake on or we'd have slid all the way back down.'

Sidney the show-off was racing round the garden on his new bike in front of his friends. He rode round without holding the handlebars. 'Look, no hands!' he shouted. Then he took his feet off the pedals. 'Look, no feet!' he shouted. He took a little longer to come round the next time, but then he came in sight. 'Look, no teeth!' shouted his friend.

Little Jimmy was saving up for his birthday. 'What would you like?' asked his dad.

'I've got my eye on that mountain bike in the shop in the High Street,' he replied.

His dad looked at the money he'd saved, and said sadly, 'Well, you'd better keep your eye on it, because at this rate you'll never get your bottom on it!'

A man went on a pilgrimage to Lourdes, and on his return, went through the 'Nothing to Declare' part of the Customs hall. The Customs officer looked at the crate of bottles he had with him. 'What's all this then?' he asked.

'Holy water,' replied the traveller.

'We'll see about that,' said the officer, opening one of the bottles and sniffing the contents. 'This smells to me like gin.'

'Heaven be praised!' cried the pilgrim, 'another miracle!'

MR TWIDDLE: When we were in China we saw a ship suspended in the air over the dock.
MR TWADDLE: Shanghai?
MR TWIDDLE: No, only a few feet above the water.

SOLLY: Can I share your skis?
MOLLY: Yes, we'll go halves.
SOLLY: Great, thanks.
MOLLY: That's all right. I'll have them going downhill and you can have them going uphill.

Why did Mr and Mrs Fusspot always take their holidays in the spring?
They liked clean sheets.

What leaves yellow footprints on the seabed?
A lemon sole.

An Eskimo mother was sitting in her igloo reading to her young son. 'Little Jack Horner sat in the corner . . .'
Her son interrupted. 'Mum, what's a corner?'

What's an ig?
An Eskimo house without a loo.

What did one Eskimo say to another?
'Ours is an ice house, ours is.'

What did the Eskimo girl do to her boyfriend?
Gave him the cold shoulder.

What's Chinese and deadly?
Chop sueycide.

Where do the Chinese make car horns?
Hong King.

AMERICAN BOY: I can pick up a cent with my toes.
ENGLISH BOY: So what? My dog can pick up a scent with his nose.

MR GOBBLE: When we travelled across the Channel from Southampton to Le Havre we had six meals.
MR GABBLE: That's rather a lot, isn't it?
MR GOBBLE: Yes, three down and three up.

A lady who'd never travelled on a ship before was unpacking in her cabin when her husband came in. 'There are lots of cupboards,' she said brightly. 'I've put all your clothes in that one over there with the round door.'
    'Oh dear,' he sighed, 'that's the porthole.'

Another passenger on the same ship was feeling very queasy as it ploughed through rough seas. He clung on to the rail, and said to a passing steward, 'I feel terrible. Whatever shall I do?'

'You'll soon find out,' replied the steward, grinning.

A young French boy was thumbing a lift on a country road in England when a car stopped. 'Do you want a lift?' asked the driver.

'Oui, oui,' replied the boy.

'Not in my car you don't!' said the driver.

A lady who'd never flown before asked the air hostess, as she settled her in her seat, 'What happens if we run out of petrol?'

'Don't worry,' replied the air hostess. 'The co-pilot gets out and pushes.'

MR DIM: I flew to the Bahamas last year.
MR DUMB: So did I.
MR DIM: Doesn't it make your arms tired?

MAN HAILING TAXI: How much to take me to the station?
CABBIE: £5, sir.
MAN: And how much for my suitcase?
CABBIE: No charge for the suitcase, sir.
MAN: OK, you take the suitcase and I'll walk.

A school party was going on a cross-Channel ferry to France and one of the teachers was running through the procedure to be followed on the boat. 'What would you do,' she asked, 'if one of the girls fell overboard?'

'Sound the alarm,' replied a pupil.

'Good,' said the teacher. 'And what would you do if one of the teachers fell overboard?'

'Er, which one, Miss?'

Mr and Mrs Dimwit had driven all the way from Leeds to Dover, loaded up with things for their camping holiday. They arrived just in time to catch their ferry to France. As they sat in the queue for boarding, Mrs Dimwit suddenly said, 'I wish we'd brought the kitchen table with us.'

'Haven't we got enough things?' said her husband, looking at the pile of luggage in the back of the car.

'Yes,' replied his wife. 'But our tickets are on the kitchen table.'

TRAIN PASSENGER: Does this train stop at Brighton?
RAILWAYMAN: If it doesn't there'll be an enormous splash.

How do you make a Mexican chilli?
Take him to the South Pole.

How do you make a Venetian blind?
Poke him in the eye.

How do you make a Maltese cross?
Steal his supper.

What's a Grecian urn?
About 100 drachmas a week.

Mr and Mrs Wobbletum were on holiday in Paris. 'Do you know,' said Mrs Wobbletum to her husband, 'we've been here a whole week and we haven't visited the Louvre yet.'

'I know,' replied her husband. 'It must be the water.'

An American tourist stopped his car and asked a local, 'Are we on the right road for Shakespeare's birthplace?'

'Yes, go straight on,' he replied. 'But you needn't hurry. He's dead, you know.'

A train in India was going very, very slowly, and a party of American tourists was growing increasingly impatient. Finally, when it stopped for about the hundredth time, one of the tourists got out, walked to the front, and asked the engine-driver, 'Can't you go any faster?'

'Oh, yes, sir,' replied the driver, 'but I'm not allowed to leave the train.'

The Nextdoors were telling their neighbours about their trip to the USA. 'When my wife saw the Grand Canyon, her face dropped a mile,' said Mr Nextdoor.

'Why, wasn't it as impressive as she'd thought?' asked his neighbour.

'No, it wasn't that,' replied Mr Nextdoor. 'She fell over the edge.'

HOTEL GUEST: Can you give me a single room and a bath, please?
RECEPTIONIST: I can give you a room but you'll have to take your own bath.

HOTEL GUEST ON PHONE: Is that Reception?
RECEPTIONIST: Yes, sir. This is the tenth time you've called. What's eating you?
HOTEL GUEST: That's what I'd like to know.

HOTEL MANAGER: And did you enjoy your stay, sir?
HOTEL GUEST: Yes, but I'm sorry to be leaving the hotel now I've practically bought it.

A couple of hikers were tramping through the countryside and lost their way, so by the time they arrived at the George and Dragon, the village pub where they'd planned to stay the night, the doors were shut and the owners had gone to bed. They knocked timidly on the door.

A head appeared at an upstairs window. 'Go away,' it shouted. 'Don't you know what time it is? We're closed.' And the window slammed shut.

Undeterred, the hikers knocked a second time. 'What is it now?' demanded the head.

'Could we speak to George this time, please?' asked one of the hikers.

Happy Families

MUM: Why is your sister crying?
JADE: Because I won't give her a piece of my chocolate.
MUM: Well, what's she done with her own chocolate?
JADE: She cried when I ate that, too.

TRUDIE: Is your mother one of those women who lie about their age?
RUDI: No. She says she's as old as Dad and then lies about his age.

HETTIE: How's your mum getting on with her diet?
BETTY: Very well. She's almost disappeared.

TIMMY: My big brother speaks five languages.
TOMMY: And he can't say 'please' or 'thank you' in any of them.

Katie's dreadful Aunt Jemima had been staying at Katie's house. One morning she said to Katie, 'I think I'll go home tomorrow. Will you be sorry?'

'Oh yes,' replied Katie.

'Why's that?' asked her aunt.

'I thought you were going today.'

DAN: My brother says he can beat any man with one hand.

ANNE: But can he find anyone to fight with one hand?

Why did the boy put his father in the fridge?
Because he wanted ice-cold pop.

'My grandfather believes in a balanced diet. He always keeps a bottle of beer in each hand.'

'My grandfather had so many candles on his birthday cake we were driven back by the heat.'

'My grandfather changed his will ten times in the last two years.'
'He's obviously a fresh heir fiend.'

HOLLY: What's your dad getting for Christmas?
POLLY: Balder.

CHRIS: Do you have a good memory for faces, Dad?
DAD: Yes, why?
CHRIS: Because I've just broken your shaving mirror.

JAMES: Do you come from a tough neighbourhood?
JOHN: I'll say. Anyone who still has his own teeth by the age of ten is a sissy.

AUNTIE CLARA: How old were you on your last birthday, Kate?
KATE: Seven.
AUNTIE CLARA: And how old will you be on your next birthday?
KATE: Nine.
AUNTIE CLARA: I don't think that's possible, you know.
KATE: Oh yes it is, because today's my birthday.

NELLIE: Where were you born?
KELLY: In the local hospital.
NELLIE: How awful! Were you ill?

NELLIE: How old is your mum?
KELLY: She says she's around 35.
NELLIE: I think she's been around it a few times.

MILLIE: We always say a prayer at my house before we eat.
TILLY: We don't need to do that at our house, my mum's a good cook.

JAYNE: What has a head and no brain but still drives?
WAYNE: Your brother?
JAYNE: Yes, but the answer is a golf club.

MUM: Wash your hands, it's nearly time for your piano lesson.
BELINDA: Don't worry, I'll only play the black notes.

DAD: You shouldn't hit a boy when he's down.
DENNIS: What do you think I got him down for?

DAD: Who gave you that black eye?
DORIS: Nobody gave it me, I had to fight for it.

MUM: Have you been fighting again? You've lost your front teeth.
JOE: No I haven't. They're in my pocket.

GILLY: That's Jerry. His mother almost lost him when he was little.
BILLY: She probably didn't take him far enough into the woods.

BERYL: Some people can cook but don't.
MERYL: My brother can't cook, but does.

JOHN: My sister should have been born in the Dark Ages.
DON: Why?
JOHN: She looks terrible in daylight.

Micky saw his big sister kissing a boy, so the next day he went up to the boy and said, 'I saw you kissing my sister Mary last night.'

'Oh dear,' said the boy. 'If I give you £1 will you promise not to tell your mum and dad?'

'It'll cost you £5,' said Micky.

'£5! That's very expensive!'

'Perhaps, but it's what all the others give me.'

COUSIN MARY: And are you a good boy, Harold?
HAROLD: No. I'm the kind of boy my mum doesn't let me play with.

MOLLY: I hear your twin brothers stick together.
POLLY: If you washed as little as they did you'd get rather sticky, too.

CAROL: Is it true that people spring from dust?
MUM: Yes.
CAROL: In that case you'd better come quickly, for under my bed is the birth of a nation.

KYLIE: My father hates to see Mum shovelling the snow.
KEVIN: What does he do about it?
KYLIE: He draws the curtains.

AUNTY EVELYN: And has your baby brother come to stay?
HELEN: I think so. He's taken all his clothes off.

AUNTY ETHEL: What's your new baby's name?
ELLIE: I don't know. He can't talk.

JENNY: Is it true my baby brother came from heaven?
MUM: Yes.
JENNY: I don't blame God for throwing him out.

JOHNNY: How old is your sister?
DONNY: One.
JOHNNY: My dog's one and he can walk twice as well as your sister.
DONNY: So he should, he's got twice as many legs.

SHARON: How did Mum know you hadn't had a bath?
DARREN: I forgot to spill water on the bathroom floor.

MUM: What's the matter, Alfred?
ALFRED: All the kids at school call me Bighead.
MUM: Never mind, love, just pop down to the greengrocer's and bring me back 10 lb of potatoes in your cap, will you?

MUM: You've got those boots on the wrong feet.
DILLY: But these are the only feet I've got.

GEMMA: My eldest brother has just passed his driving test.
EMMA: Good for him.
GEMMA: And good for us, too, because it means we can all move up one bike.

MUM: Eat up your vegetables, Jemima, they're good for growing children.
JEMIMA: But who wants to grow children?

MUM: Don't eat your food so quickly, Kenny.
KENNY: But I might lose my appetite if I don't.

Tommy was out for a meal with his mum and dad and sister Tina. Tina was very young, and didn't eat much of her food. 'Never mind,' said Mum. 'It will do for lunch tomorrow.' So when the waiter came, Dad asked for a bag to take the leftovers home for the dog.

'Oh, Dad,' said Tommy, 'are we getting a dog?'

'Mum, Dad's just fallen off the roof.'
'I know, I saw him go past the window.'

BEN: Parents shouldn't have children. They don't understand them.
KEN: Why do you say that?
BEN: Well, they put me to bed when I'm wide awake and get me up when I'm still asleep.

MRS TWIDDLE: When I got home last night my son had a blazing fire going.
MRS TWADDLE: That's nice.
MRS TWIDDLE: It wasn't, actually. You see, we don't have a fireplace.

MOTHER: My hair is going grey.
MERVYN: Why?
MOTHER: I expect it's because you're so naughty. You
tire me out.
**MERVYN: Oh, Mum, you must have been really
awful to Grandma.**

MANDY: What does your mother do if she feels ill?
ANDY: Sends me to your house to play.

The vicar found two boys fighting. He got hold of one by
his collar and pulled him away from the other boy. 'You
mustn't fight, you know. You must love your enemy.'
    'But he's not my enemy,' said the angry little tyke.
'He's my brother.'

HARRY: Did you meet your father at the station?
LARRY: Oh, no, I've known him for years.

MRS HOUSEWIFE: One more word from you and I'm
going home to mother.
MR HOUSEWIFE: Taxi!

DAD: Do you like moving pictures?
DENNIS: Oh yes.
DAD: Good, you can help me carry some upstairs.

FREDA: My uncle's got a memory like an elephant.
FREDDIE: And the shape to go with it!

MUM: Scrape that mud off your shoes before you come in here, Harold.
HAROLD: But, Mum, I'm not wearing any shoes.

MRS BARREL: I was sorry to hear that your house had blown away in that hurricane – and with your mother-in-law still inside it.
MRS BURRELL: Oh, well, she'd kept saying she wanted a holiday.

LAURIE: I hear Dennis's family are sending him to his penfriend by the sea for the summer.
LALLIE: Does he need a holiday?
LAURIE: No, but his parents do.

LINDA: My brother and I had a great time on holiday by the sea. We took turns to bury each other in the sand.
LAURA: Sounds fun.
LINDA: It was. And next year we're going back to dig him up.

'Mummy, Mummy, why do I keep going round in circles?'
'Shut up or I'll nail your other foot to the floor.'

'Dad, Mum says to tell you she's going out.'
'Pour more petrol on her, then.'

'Mummy, Mummy, why do you keep poking Daddy in the ribs?'
'Because if I don't the fire will go out.'

What's old, pink and wrinkled and belongs to Grandma?
Grandpa.

Little Susie was given a harmonica and a bottle of perfume for her birthday. That day the vicar and his wife dropped in for tea, and Susie sat between them. She smiled at them as they sipped their tea and ate their cucumber sandwiches, and said brightly, 'If you hear a little noise, and smell a little smell, it's me.'

BEN: One of my relatives died at Waterloo.
KEN: Really? Which platform?

MRS BROWN: At last my husband's found a hobby.
MRS GREEN: But is it a hobby he can stick to?
MRS BROWN: Oh, I think so.
MRS GREEN: What does he do?
MRS BROWN: He spends all evening glued to the television.

TRACEY: What a lovely jumper.
STACEY: It's a hunting jumper.
TRACEY: Why's it called that?
STACEY: Because my sister will be hunting for it.

BOBBIE: We had a letter from my brother the other day.
NOBBY: What did he say?
BOBBIE: That he'd grown another foot.
NOBBY: Good gracious! What did your mum say?
BOBBIE: She thought she'd better knit him another sock.

DAVE: Do you live in a tough neighbourhood?
MAVE: I'll say! When I hung up my Christmas stocking Father Christmas stole it!

JENNY: My brother and I know every word in the English language.
BENNY: Do you? Tell me what 'bighead' means, then.
JENNY: My brother knows that one.

DEPARTMENT STORE SANTA: And what would you like for Christmas?
NAUGHTY NIGEL: I told you in the letter Dad posted last week – you can't have forgotten already!

PADDY: John's dad looks pretty old.
PERRY: That's an understatment. When he was a boy history was called current affairs.

'My auntie wasn't lying when she said she'd turned 35. She did, about 100 years ago!'

How do you tell an old person from a young person?
An old person can sing and brush their teeth at the same time.

DILLY: I'm going to give you a china teapot for Christmas.
MUM: But I've got one already.
DILLY: No you haven't, I just dropped it.

BEN: There's a man at the door collecting for the new school swimming-pool.
DAD: Here's a glass of water, give him that.

KEN: There's a man at the door collecting for the old folks' home.
DAD: Give him Granny.

JIMMY: The careers teacher said that with a mind like mine I should study criminal law.
DAD: Well done, son, I'm proud of you.
JIMMY: Yes, he said I had a criminal mind.

Monstrous Mirth

What's a dragon's favourite party game?
Swallow my leader.

How does a witch tell the time?
With a witch-watch.

What's a witch's favourite kind of music?
Hagtime.

What do you call a wizard on a broomstick?
A flying sorcerer.

What does a racing witch ride?
A broom-broom-stick.

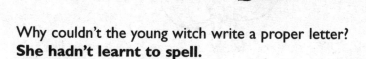

Why couldn't the young witch write a proper letter?
She hadn't learnt to spell.

How does a werewolf sign a letter?
'Best vicious.'

Why was the werewolf in the launderette?
It was a wash 'n' werewolf.

'Mum, what's a vampire?'
'Shut up and drink your soup before it clots.'

Where does a vampire keep his money?
In the blood bank.

What did the polite vampire say to the dentist after
having a tooth filled?
'Fangs a lot.'

Why do vampires use mouthwash?
To stop bat breath.

Whom did the vampire marry?
The girl necks door.

FIRST VAMPIRE: A tramp stopped me in the street and
said he hadn't had a bite in days.
SECOND VAMPIRE: What did you do?
FIRST VAMPIRE: I bit him, of course.

Are vampires crazy?
Well, lots of them are bats.

What's a vampire's favourite dance?
The fangdango.

What do you call a thick vampire?
A stupid clot.

Why was Count Dracula keen to help young vampires?
He liked to see new blood in the business.

What was Dracula's favourite breakfast cereal?
Ready-neck.

Why didn't Dracula marry?
He was a confirmed bat-chelor.

How do you join Dracula's fan club?
Send your name, address and blood group.

What kind of ship did Dracula sail in?
A blood vessel.

How can you tell when Dracula is angry?
He flips his lid.

Why is it so easy to play tricks on vampires?
Because they're all suckers.

Did you hear about the two vampires who were
forbidden to marry?
They loved in vein.

What does a vampire do when he's tired?
Takes a coffin break.

Why do you never see a fat vampire?
They eat necks to nothing.

What do you call a vampire who stays out all night?
A fresh air fiend.

What do phantom football supporters sing?
'Here we ghost, here we ghost, here we ghost . . .'

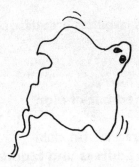

What would you do if you saw three monsters walking
down the road?
Hope they were going to a fancy dress party.

What's a sea monster's favourite supper?
Fish and ships.

What monster is a real cool guy?
The abominable snowman.

Why was the abominable snowman comedian a failure?
His jokes weren't so hot.

Why didn't the abominable snowman have many friends?
He gave people the cold shoulder.

Why didn't the abominable snowman apply for a job?
He got cold feet.

How do monster snowmen feel when they melt?
Abominable.

What's a monster's favourite ballet?
Swamp Lake.

Why did the monster stop playing with his brother?
He got tired of kicking him around.

Did you hear about the boy monster and the girl
monster?
They fell in love at first fright.

How does a monster count up to 23?
On its fingers.

How do you greet a three-headed monster?
'Hello, hello, hello.'

FIRST MONSTER: That girl rolled her eyes at me.
SECOND MONSTER: Well, roll them back again.

SIGN IN A MONSTER'S PARLOUR: Home is where you
hang your head.

How did Frankenstein's monster eat his dinner?
He bolted it down.

MONSTER MUM, ADDRESSING HER DAUGHTER:
Don't look out of the window, Doreen, everyone will
think it's Hallowe'en.

Did you hear about the girl monster who wasn't pretty
and wasn't ugly?
She was pretty ugly.

HARRY: What would you do if a monster came in your
front door?
LARRY: Run out of the back door.

What does a monster do if he loses a hand?
Goes to a second-hand shop.

Who won the Monster Beauty Contest?
Nobody.

What would you call a beautiful monster?
A failure.

What do monsters sing at Christmas?
'Deck the halls with poison ivy . . .'

What's a gargoyle?
Something a monster takes for a sore throat.

What's a monster's favourite dessert?
Leeches and scream.

Why did the baby monster push his dad's finger in the light socket?
Because he wanted fizzy pop.

And Then There Was the One About . . .

One day Tommy Tortoise was taken out for tea by his parents. They went into a cafe, and Mrs Tortoise ordered tea and cakes, Mr Tortoise ordered egg sandwiches, and Tommy ordered ice-cream. He was just about to start eating it when his father said, 'Oh dear, I seem to have forgotten my wallet. Would you pop home and fetch it please, Tommy.'

Tommy was a very well-behaved tortoise who always did what his parents asked. So instead of eating his ice-cream, he headed for the door.

Two days later, he still hadn't returned. His father turned to his mother, and said, 'I think, my dear, we'd better eat Tommy's ice-cream before it melts.'

Whereupon a voice from the doorway called out, 'If you do that, I won't go.'

A tribe who lived in a remote part of Africa in huts made of mud and thatch once found a beautiful golden throne in the middle of the jungle. They took it home, and built it a special hut, and people came from far and wide to marvel at it.

Then the rainy season began, and it rained and rained day after day and night after night. The headman decided he'd better see if the throne was all right, so he went to check on it. To his horror, he discovered it was completely covered in a slimy green mould. Feeling very depressed, he walked out of the hut and into the rain, where he found the witch doctor was waiting for him.

'What's the matter?' he asked the headman.

So the headman explained what had happened to the throne.

'It just goes to show,' said the witch doctor, ' that people who live in grass houses shouldn't store thrones.'

A luxury liner which spent its time taking very rich people on Mediterranean cruises had a theatre in which various celebrated artistes performed every night. One of them was a very clever magician, who amazed everyone with his talents. Everyone, that is, except a parrot that belonged to a member of the crew. Although banned from the theatre, the parrot managed to find a way in every time the magician was performing and would screech, 'It's a con! It's all done by mirrors!' until it was removed from the scene.

One dark night a storm rolled in from the east. The wind blew, the rain fell in torrents, and mountainous waves crashed over the deck of the ship. With a great juddering crash the ship broke in two, and sank without trace. All that remained were a few pieces of floating wood, and by a strange chance, on one of these clung the magician and the parrot.

The latter looked at the magician with a new respect. 'OK, wise guy,' he said. 'I'll grant you that was pretty good. But tell me, what did you do with the ship?'

One night in the old Wild West a group of cowboys were sitting round a camp fire exchanging stories. As the night wore on these got wilder and wilder, and no one believed them. 'I know an Indian chief,' said one of the cowboys, 'who never forgets a single thing anyone ever says to him.'

The others didn't believe him.

'It's true,' vowed the cowboy. 'The devil take my soul if it isn't.'

The devil happened to be listening, so he appeared to the cowboy and asked to be taken to meet this amazing Indian.

'Fine,' said the cowboy. 'Let's go.' So off they travelled,

and rode many miles until they came to the Indian
reservation. The cowboy introduced the devil to the
Indian chief.

'Do you like beans?' asked the devil.

'Yes,' replied the chief.

Many years later the cowboy died, and the devil set
out to find the Indian, so he could claim the cowboy's
soul. The Indian was by this time a very old man, and the
devil greeted him in Indian fashion, by holding up his
hand and saying, 'How.'

'On toast,' replied the Indian.

Fishermen have a reputation for telling tall tales, and one
who lived in a village on the west coast of Ireland was
particularly well known for it. No matter how many fish
he caught, nor how big they were, every time he came
home from a fishing trip he would tell everyone about
the huge and amazing fish he almost caught.

The fisherman and his wife had two sons, known by
the nicknames of Home and Away, because of their
fondness for watching football on the telly. One fine day
he took them out fishing with him.

They were late back, and the fisherman's wife was
getting worried. She was even more upset when her
husband walked into the house alone.

'Oh, Sarah,' he said. 'The most terrible thing has
happened. An enormous fish – it must have been ten
metres long – reached up over the side of the boat and
swallowed poor Home whole!'

'Oh dear,' sobbed his wife. 'Oh poor, dear Home!
Whatever shall we do?'

'But I'm afraid that's only part of what happened,'

sighed the fisherman. 'You should have seen the size of the fish that got Away!'

A violinist wanted to test his theory that music could tame wild animals. So he went off to Africa and in a clearing in the jungle, began to play.

At first nothing happened, but then an elephant strolled up. It sat down, and began to wave its trunk in time to the music. Then a lion appeared. At first it growled, but as it listened, it began to purr like a cat. A hippo waddled out of the river and lay down to listen, a dreamy smile on its face. Birds stopped singing in the trees, and monkeys sat quietly. All the creatures seemed enchanted.

Then a crocodile climbed out of the river, opened its massive jaws, and gulp! swallowed the violinist in one go.

'Why did you do that?' asked the other animals. 'We were enjoying his music!'

The crocodile put its front leg up to its ear. 'Pardon?' it said.

Two friends sat in front of the TV to watch Sheffield United play Aston Villa on Match of the Day. 'I bet you £5 United wins,' said Bill.

'OK,' said Ben. 'I'll bet you £5 that Villa wins.'

'Done!' said Bill.

They watched the match, in which there was no score until the last few minutes and then United scored a splendid goal. 'There you are,' said Bill. 'I told you!'

'OK,' said Ben, fishing in his pocket. 'I owe you £5.'

'Actually,' said Bill, 'I've a confession to make. I can't take your £5. I knew United would win. I heard the result earlier.'

'So did I,' said Ben. 'But I didn't think Villa would play so badly they would lose a second time.'

A vicar was playing golf with one of his parishioners, and the man was having an off day. At the first green he missed an easy putt. 'Damn!' he exclaimed. 'I've missed!'

The vicar raised an eyebrow but said nothing. At the second green the man missed again. 'Damn, I've missed!' he exclaimed again. And so it went on. The man kept missing his shots, and cursing loudly.

Finally the vicar could stand it no longer. 'I must ask you to moderate your language,' he said. 'Or the Lord may strike you down.'

At that moment a big black cloud rolled overhead, and a jagged flash of lightning struck the vicar. From out of the cloud came a deep voice, 'Damn! I've missed!'

Food for Thought

What's the main ingredient in dog biscuits?
Collie flour.

What's white on the outside, black on the inside and slippery when you eat it?
A slug sandwich.

What's brown on the outside, black on the inside and slippery when you eat it?
A slug sandwich on wholemeal bread.

What do you call two rows of cabbages?
A dual cabbageway.

TILLY: I'm going to order a double portion of chips.
MILLIE: A double portion? Isn't that expensive?
TILLY: I don't know, but it's certainly expansive.

Which vegetables are found in the loo?
Leeks and peas.

JIMMY: What's the difference between a cowpat and a chocolate ice-cream?
TIMMY: I don't know.
JIMMY: I'm not coming to tea at your house again, then!

'Waiter! This dinner's half cold!'
'Then eat the half that's hot.'

GRANNY: If you eat your spinach you'll grow up into a beautiful young woman.
GILLIE: Why didn't you eat your spinach when you were a girl, Gran?

FATTY: I believe in a balanced diet.
THINNY: Is that why you always have a sandwich in each hand?

Did you hear about the man who lived entirely on prunes?
The bottom dropped out of his world.

'Waiter, is this English bacon or Danish bacon?'
'Do you want to eat it or talk to it?'

What do chiropodists eat for breakfast?
Shredded feet.

What do chiropodists who don't like shredded feet eat for breakfast?
Corn flakes.

ANNIE: Did you hear about the idiot who tried to bake a birthday cake in the oven?
DANNY: No, what happened?
ANNIE: The candles melted.

Why don't the Chinese eat custard?
Have you ever tried eating custard with chopsticks?

A waitress was serving Mrs Gobble with a cup of tea. 'It looks like rain,' she observed.
Mrs Gobble sipped the tea. 'It tastes like it too,' she agreed.

NEWSFLASH: Several crates of prunes and sacks of bran have been stolen from a warehouse. Police say the thieves are still on the run.

GLORIA: Every time Graham takes me out for a meal he eats his head off.
GEORGINA: Never mind, he looks better that way.

MUM: How many times do I have to tell you to stay away from the mince pies?
DENNIS: Never again, Mum, I just ate the last one.

What's yellow and writes?
A ballpoint banana.

SALLY: Sarah looks large, but they say she's a light eater.
WALLY: Yes, as soon as it's light she starts eating.

MR WIBBLE: That restaurant in the High Street serves chicken that really tickles the palate.
MR WOBBLE: What do they do to it?
MR WIBBLE: They leave the feathers on.

Why is hot toast like a caterpillar?
It's the grub that makes the butter fly.

How do you make an apple puff?
Chase it round the garden.

How do you make an apple turnover?
Pull the sheets off it.

What can a whole apple do that half an apple can't do?
Look round.

How do you make a Swiss roll?
Push him off an Alp.

What's worse than biting a strawberry and finding a worm?
Biting a strawberry and finding half a worm.

JOHNNY: Do you like baked apples?
DAD: Yes. Why?
JOHNNY: The orchard's on fire.

What's yellow and goes 'buzz'?
An electric banana.

What's yellow and points north?
A magnetic banana.

'Gerry's so unlucky that when he bought some bananas they were empty.'

Two old men were going on a train journey for the first time. Just before they left, a friend gave them some bananas to eat on the journey. They'd never eaten bananas before, either.

They sat for a while, chatting and watching the scenery go by. Then the first man decided he'd try one of the bananas. Just as he took the first bite, the train went into a tunnel.

'Have you tried these bananas?' he asked his friend.

'No,' he replied.

'Well, don't,' said the first man. 'I took one bite and went blind.'

How do you make a banana split?
Cut it in half.

What looks just like half a sausage?
The other half.

MR SMITH: Why can't you make bread like my mother?
MRS SMITH: I would if you could make dough like your father.

MUM: What did I say I'd do to you if you ate the Christmas cake?
SUSIE: My memory must be as bad as yours, I can't remember.

TRACEY: He likes to have intimate little dinners for two.
STACEY: Trouble is, no one eats them except him.

What's green and goes 'boing, boing'?
Spring cabbage.

SHOPPER: How much are your ducks?
BUTCHER: £1.20 a pound.
SHOPPER: Did you raise them yourself?
BUTCHER: Yes, yesterday they were £1 a pound.

Which cake wanted to rule the world?
Attila the Bun.

What do elves have for tea?
Fairy cakes.

What did the cannibal say when he saw his wife chopping
up a snake and a little man?
'Oh, no, not snake and pygmy pie again!'

What happened when the cannibals ate a comedian?
They had a feast of fun.

What's a cannibal's favourite wine?
One with lots of body!

Why was the cannibal child thrown out of school?
He kept buttering up the teacher.

Why did the cannibals find the missionary indigestible?
You can't keep a good man down.

'Mummy, mummy, I don't like Uncle Charlie!'
**'Then leave him at the side of your plate, dear,
and just eat your chips.'**

What *is* a cannibal?
Someone who is fed up with people.

How do the Welsh eat cheese?
Caerphilly.

What's made of chocolate and found in the sea?
An oyster egg.

JOHN: What's the difference between a bar of chocolate
and a pile of horse manure?
DON: I don't know.
JOHN: In that case I'll eat the chocolate and you can
have the horse manure.

MRS WHITE: How much are those cabbages?
GREENGROCER: 55p for two or 35p for one.
MRS WHITE: Here's 20p, I'll have the other one.

What happened when the Swede died?
There was a huge turnip at his funeral.

Kate and Clare went into a cafe and ordered two glasses
of orangeade. When the waitress brought them, they
each took out a packet of sandwiches and began to eat.
    'Hey!' said the waitress. 'You can't eat your own food
in here, you know.'
    So the two girls swapped sandwiches.

TINA: Is it correct to eat chicken legs with your fingers?
GINA: No, fingers should be eaten separately.

What goes up brown or white and comes down yellow
and white?
An egg.

What do you call a mischievous egg?
A practical yolker.

FIRST BOILED EGG IN PAN: Phew! It's hot in here.
**SECOND BOILED EGG IN PAN: It gets worse –
when you get out they bash your head in.**

DUMB DONNA: I've heard egg shampoo is good for the hair.
**DIZZY DORA: How do you get a hen to lay an
egg on your head?**

JIM: Did you hear the joke about the eggs?
TIM: No.
JIM: Two bad.

What did the egg in the monastery say?
'Out of the frying-pan, into the friar.'

Why did Ronald McDonald go to the optician?
He kept seeing double cheeseburgers.

Why do idiots hate eating chicken broth?
They can't get it to stay on the fork.

ALGY: This soup is terrible.
ANDY: Why do you say that?
ALGY: A little swallow told me.

JENNY: I feel like a cup of tea.
**KENNY: You look like one, too, all wet and
sloppy.**

What kind of potatoes go, 'Oui, oui, buzz, buzz'?
French flies.

Did you hear about the man who was so lazy he invented an edible sandwich bag so you don't have to unpack your lunch?

What's a goat's favourite food?
Alphabutt soup.

What vegetable has trouble breathing?
Asparagasp.

BELLA: Let's eat fruit and watch a horror movie.
HER FELLER: Why?
BELLA: I want to eat peaches and scream.

MARGARINE: How old are you?
SLICE OF BREAD: Old enough to know butter.

What's the best place to be if you're the ham in a sandwich?
Home in bread.

What did the biscuits say to the almonds?
'You're nuts and we're crackers.'

What does a vegetarian vicar say before dinner?
'Lettuce pray.'

Why is a hot dog the best of all dogs?
Because it feeds the hand that bites it.

What do you call an extra long hot dog?
A frank-further.

What's Italian, 50 metres high and good to eat?
The leaning tower of pizza.

What's the best veg to have with jacket potatoes?
Button mushrooms.

How do you make a lemon drop?
Shake the tree hard.

MUM: Why is that book in the saucepan?
DIM DINAH: It says 'Cookbook' so I did.

ANGRY SHOPPER: There was a bluebottle on that fruit
cake I bought yesterday.
**BAKER: Well, bring it back and I'll exchange it for
a currant.**

CLARENCE: I've heard fish is good for the brain.
CUTHBERT: So have I, I eat it every day.
CLARENCE: It's just an old wives' tale, then.

A man was eating dinner in a restaurant when he
sneezed violently. His false teeth shot out, hit the wall
opposite, and broke in pieces.

'Oh dear,' he mumbled, 'Whatever shall I do?'

'Don't worry,' said the waiter. 'My brother will fix you
up with a new set. Just wait here a few minutes while I
give him a ring.'

Sure enough, the man turned up a few minutes later
with a new set of teeth that fitted the diner perfectly.
The waiter came along to check how he was doing.

'Fine,' smiled the diner. 'They fit very well. Your
brother is a very clever dentist.'

'No,' replied the waiter, 'He's not a dentist. He's an undertaker.'

Why don't grapes snore?
They don't want to wake the rest of the bunch.

What kind of motorbike can cook eggs?
A scrambler.

Cindy was helping her mum chop up vegetables for a stew. 'Mind your fingers,' said her mum. 'Remember most accidents happen in the kitchen.'
'I know,' sighed Cindy. 'I have to eat them.'

The pilot of a light aircraft was flying over the jungle when his engine failed. Before the plane crashed he managed to get out and parachute down, only to land in a cannibal's cooking pot.
    'Hullo,' said the cannibal chief. 'What's this flier doing in my soup?'

What's the best thing to put in a fruit pie?
Your teeth.

How did rich vegetables used to travel?
By horse and cabbage.

Why was the mushroom invited to lots of parties?
He was a fungi to be with.

Why aren't bananas ever lonely?
They hang around in bunches.

What keeps hot in the fridge?
Mustard.

What's round, orange and can't sit down?
A seatless satsuma.

What's the difference between a nightwatchman and a butcher?
One stays awake; the other weighs a steak.

What's yellow, soft, and goes round and round?
A long-playing omelette.

A man was standing at a bus-stop eating fish and chips when a lady with a dog walked up. The bus was a long time arriving, and the dog was watching the man hungrily. 'Do you mind if I throw him a bit?' the man asked the lady.

'Not at all,' she replied.

So the man picked up the dog and threw him over someone's garden wall.

Can an orange box?
No, but a tomato can.

What's the best day to have
bacon for breakfast?
Fry-day.

'Waiter, will my omelette be long?'
'No, sir, round.'

A sailor and his pet parrot were once shipwrecked on a desert island. There was nothing to eat, and the sailor didn't even manage to catch fish from the sea. So, although he hated the idea, he was forced to eat his parrot.

Not long afterwards he was rescued, and explained how he'd survived.

'What did the parrot taste like?' asked his rescuer.

'Chicken, goose, duck – that bird could imitate anything,' replied the sailor.

How many peas are there in a pint?
Just one!

A market gardener went out one day and found a boy climbing one of his apple trees. 'And what do you think you're doing?' he asked the lad.

'Er, one of your apples fell down so I climbed up to put it back,' explained the boy.

Susie was helping her mum lay the table. 'Have you put the pepper in the pepperpot?' asked her mother.

'No, Mum,' replied Susie. 'I can't get it through all those little holes.'

What do you call hamburgers with cinnamon, ginger and nutmeg that sing pop songs?
The Spice Grils.

How do pixies eat?
By goblin.

Why is roast pork like an old radio?
Both have lots of crackling.

What peels and chips but never cracks?
A potato.

SHOPPER: Those potatoes you sold me were full of eyes.
GREENGROCER: Well, you did say you wanted enough to see you through the week.

Sign Language

SIGN ON A ROPE FACTORY:
Knot your ordinary company.

SIGN ON AN AIR CONDITIONING FACTORY:
We show people how to chill out.

SIGN IN A HOTEL IN NORWAY:
Ladies are requested not to have children in the bar.

SIGN IN A HOTEL IN PARIS:
Please leave your values at the desk.

SIGN IN A ZOO: Please do not feed the animals. If you
have suitable food, please give it to the guard on duty.

SIGN IN A CAFE: Special today – no ice-cream.

ADVERTISEMENT FOR A FOREIGN BUS COMPANY:
The comfort on our vehicles is next to none.

SIGN IN A CAFE: People are requested not to occupy
seats in this cafe if they do not intend to consume them.

SIGN IN A HOTEL CORRIDOR:
In case of fire, warm the chambermaid.

SIGN BY A SPANISH SWIMMING POOL: Bathers must
be fully dressed on entry into the pool and fully dressed
on leaving the pool.

SIGN IN A SHOE SHOP:
Boots and shoes polished inside.

SIGN IN A BARBER'S SHOP:
Hair cut while you wait.

SIGN ON A BUTCHER'S SHOP:
Pleased to meet you and meat to please you.

SIGN IN A HAIRDRESSER'S:
We curl up and dye for you.

ON A CHURCH NOTICEBOARD: Will those who have relatives buried in graves in the churchyard please keep them in order.

FOR SALE: Ming vase, property of a lady, only slightly cracked.

FOR SALE: 1936 Rolls Royce hearse. Original body.

FOR SALE: Thatched cottage. Two beds, living-room, kitchen, bathroom two miles from Stratford-on-Avon.

128

FOR SALE: Two-seater sofa. Converts to double bed. Covered in mustard.

FOR SALE: Silk wedding-dress. Only worn twice.

FOR SALE: Gentleman's antique pistols. Gentleman no further use.

TO LET: One-bedroom, fully furnished flat. £300 per month. Electricity and rats included.

CLEANER required, two hours a day, to clean small officers.

FOR SALE: Boy's bicycle, also two girls, in perfect order.

PROPERTY: Landlord has several flats let to tenants he wishes to dispose of.

YOUNG WOMAN seeks cleaning, three days a week.

WIDOWS made to your own specifications.

TO LET: Two-bedroom flat, would suit two business ladies, use of shared kitchen and bathroom or two gentlemen.

TO LET: Small mouse.

FOR SALE: Granite-faced gentleman's country house.

ADVERTISEMENT: Since taking your pills I have felt like a new woman (original may be seen on request).

ADVERTISEMENT: Rings by post. State size or enclose tape tied round finger.

SHOP SIGN: Hundreds of bargains! Why go elsewhere and be robbed when you can come here!

WANTED: The Cosy Cafe seeks person to wash dishes and two waitresses.

BAY TREE RESTAURANT -- where good food is an unexpected pleasure.

ROLLS ROYCE FOR SALE. Only one owner, dark green in colour.

SHOP SIGN: Girls ready to wear clothes.

SIGN AT A RAILWAY STATION: Toilets out of order. Please use platforms 6 and 7.

NOTICE IN A CHEMIST'S SHOP: We dispense with accuracy.

NOTICE IN AN OFFICE: Staff are requested to empty and rinse out teapots then stand upside-down on the draining-board.

SIGN IN A DRY CLEANER'S: Customers leaving garments for longer than four weeks will be disposed of.

SIGN IN A CORNISH DAIRY: Buy our superior cream – it can't be beaten!

SIGN AT A PLANT NURSERY: We always have thyme for you.

SIGN IN A FAN-MAKER'S: Working here is a breeze.

SIGN IN A GLOVE-MAKER'S: Please give us a hand.

SIGN IN A PET SHOP: Buy a dog – get one flea.

SIGN IN AN AMERICAN PERFUME FACTORY: Our work is all dollars and scents.

Knock, Knock

Knock, knock.
Who's there?
Dishes.
Dishes who?
Dishes me, open up!

Knock, knock.
Who's there?
Arfer.
Arfer who?
Arfer Gott.

Knock, knock.
Who's there?
Sonia.
Sonia who?
Sonia foot, I can smell it from here!

Knock, knock.
Who's there?
Eileen.
Eileen who?
Eileen Don your bell and broke it.

Knock, knock.
Who's there?
Wicked.
Wicked who?
Wicked make beautiful music together.

Knock, knock.
Who's there?
Howard.
Howard who?
Howard I know?

Knock, knock.
Who's there?
Betty.
Betty who?
Betty let me in, it's freezing out here!

Knock, knock.
Who's there?
Tank.
Tank who?
You're welcome.

Knock, knock.
Who's there?
Signor.
Signor who?
Signor light on so I knocked.

Knock, knock.
Who's there?
Felix.
Felix who?
Felix my ice-cream again I'll bop him one.

Knock, knock.
Who's there?
Orson.
Orson who?
Orson cart.

Knock, knock.
Who's there?
Barbara.
Barbara who?
Barbara black sheep, have you any wool?

Knock, knock.
Who's there?
Yolanda.
Yolanda who?
Yolanda me your bike? I've got a puncture.

Knock, knock.
Who's there?
Arch.
Arch who?
Bless you!

Knock, knock.
Who's there?
Ahab.
Ahab who?
Ahab to go to the loo, please let me in!

Knock, knock.
Who's there?
Nicholas.
Nicholas who?
Nicholas girls shouldn't climb ladders.

Knock, knock.
Who's there?
Olive.
Olive who?
Olive round the corner.

Knock, knock.
Who's there?
Disc.
Disc who?
Disc is a recorded message.

Knock, knock.
Who's there?
Anna.
Anna who?
Anna nother thing, how many times do I have to tell you not to knock on my door?

Knock, knock.
Who's there?
Allocate.
Allocate who?
Allocate, how are you, dear?

Knock, knock.
Who's there?
Stan.
Stan who?
Stan back, I'm coming in.

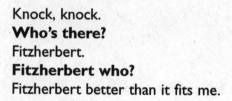

Knock, knock.
Who's there?
Fitzherbert.
Fitzherbert who?
Fitzherbert better than it fits me.

Knock, knock.
Who's there?
Matthew.
Matthew who?
Matthew lathe ith undone.

Knock, knock.
Who's there?
Cynthia.
Cynthia who?
Cynthia've been away a lot's happened.

Knock, knock.
Who's there?
Phyllis.
Phyllis who?
Phyllis in on the news.

Knock, knock.
Who's there?
Freddie.
Freddie who?
Freddie or not, I'm coming in!

Knock, knock.
Who's there?
Euripides.
Euripides who?
Euripides trousers, you buy me a new pair.

Knock, knock.
Who's there?
Eddie.
Eddie who?
Eddie body home?

Knock, knock.
Who's there?
Andy.
Andy who?
Andy little gadgets, door knockers.

Knock, knock.
Who's there?
Ammonia.
Ammonia who?
Ammonia little girl and I can't reach the doorbell.

Knock, knock.
Who's there?
Ewan.
Ewan who?
No one, just me.

Knock, knock.
Who's there?
Wooden shoe.
Wooden shoe who?
Wooden shoe like to know!

Knock, knock.
Who's there?
Annie.
Annie who?
Annie versary.

Knock, knock.
Who's there?
Warren.
Warren who?
Warren my best clothes today.

Knock, knock.
Who's there?
Mandy.
Mandy who?
Mandy lifeboats, we're sinking.

Knock, knock.
Who's there?
Spider.
Spider who?
Spider when she thought I wasn't looking.

Knock, knock.
Who's there?
Ivan.
Ivan who?
Ivan new coat, do you like it?

Knock, knock.
Who's there?
Norma Lee.
Norma Lee who?
Norma Lee we play at my house but today I've come to yours.

Knock, knock.
Who's there?
Jaws.
Jaws who?
Jaws truly.

Knock, knock.
Who's there?
Juno.
Juno who?
I dunno, Juno?

Knock, knock.
Who's there?
Bernadette.
Bernadette who?
Bernadette my sandwiches, I'm starving.

Knock, knock.
Who's there?
Datsun.
Datsun who?
Datsun old joke!

Knock, knock.
Who's there?
Hammond.
Hammond who?
Hammond eggs.

Knock, knock.
Who's there?
Alison.
Alison who?
Alison to my Walkman on the way to school.

Knock, knock.
Who's there?
Bertha.
Bertha who?
Happy Bertha-day!

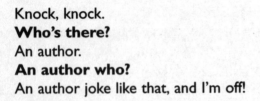

Knock, knock.
Who's there?
Pencil.
Pencil who?
Pencil fall down if the elastic breaks.

Knock, knock.
Who's there?
An author.
An author who?
An author joke like that, and I'm off!

Knock, knock.
Who's there?
Les.
Les who?
Les go out and play.

Knock, knock.
Who's there?
Kermit.
Kermit who?
Kermit a crime and you'll go to jail.

Knock, knock.
Who's there?
Dishes.

Dishes who?
Dishes the police, open up!

Knock, knock.
Who's there?
Butter.
Butter who?
Butter be quick, I'm late for school.

Knock, knock.
Who's there?
Mickey.
Mickey who?
Mickey's stuck in the lock, please open the door.

Knock, knock.
Who's there?
Sarah.
Sarah who?
Sarah nother way into this house?

Knock, knock.
Who's there?
Isabel.
Isabel who?
Isabel ringing?

Knock, knock.
Who's there?
Althea.
Althea who?
Althea later.

Knock, knock.
Who's there?
Thayer.
Thayer who?
Thayer thorry and I'll go away.

Knock, knock.
Who's there?
Willy.
Willy who?
Willy make it? Bet he won't!

Knock, knock.
Who's there?
Tamara.
Tamara who?
Tamara I'll come and see you again.

Knock, knock.
Who's there?
Oscar.
Oscar who?
Oscar if she'll let me in.

Knock, knock.
Who's there?
Mabel.
Mabel who?
Mabel doesn't work, either.

Knock, knock.
Who's there?
Justin.
Justin who?
Justin time for lunch.

Knock, knock.
Who's there?
Colin.
Colin who?
Colin and see me sometime.

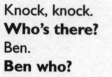

Knock, knock.
Who's there?
Ben.
Ben who?
Ben waiting out here for ages!

Knock, knock.
Who's there?
Andrew.
Andrew who?
Andrew a picture of our teacher on the wall.

Knock, knock.
Who's there?
Auto.
Auto who?
Auto know, but I don't.

Knock, knock.
Who's there?
Gus.
Gus who?
That's what you're supposed to do!

Knock, knock.
Who's there?
Waddle.
Waddle who?
Waddle you give me to go away?

Knock, knock.
Who's there?
Midas.
Midas who?
Midas well let me in.

Knock, knock.
Who's there?
Howie.
Howie who?
Howie Dewin?

Knock, knock.
Who's there?
Lee King.
Lee King who?
Lee King roof's a nuisance.

Knock, knock.
Who's there?
Snow.
Snow who?
Snow use, I can't remember.

Knock, knock.
Who's there?
Dunce.
Dunce who?
Dunce A. another word.

Knock, knock.
Who's there?
Scott.
Scott who?
Scott nothing to do with you.

Knock, knock.
Who's there?
Tennessee.
Tennessee who?
Tennessee you tonight?

Knock, knock.
Who's there?
Abyssinia.
Abyssinia who?
Abyssinia soon.

Knock, knock.
Who's there?
Havana.
Havana who?
Havana wonderful time, wish you were here.

Knock, knock.
Who's there?
Francis.
Francis who?
Francis where people speak French.

Knock, knock.
Who's there?
Europe.
Europe who?
Europe to no good again.

Knock, knock.
Who's there?
Money.
Money who?
Money hurts since I twisted it playing football.

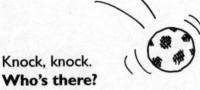

Knock, knock.
Who's there?
Aida.
Aida who?
Aida too many sweets and now I feel sick!

Knock, knock.
Who's there?
Venice.
Venice who?
Venice the next train to London?

Knock, knock.
Who's there?
Worzel.
Worzel who?
First on the right at the top of the stairs.

Knock, knock.
Who's there?
Statue.
Statue who?
Statue? This is me.

Knock, knock.
Who's there?
Ooze.
Ooze who?
Ooze eaten all the jam tarts?

Knock, knock.
Who's there?
Sofa.
Sofa who?
Sofa, so good.

Knock, knock.
Who's there?
Zizi.
Zizi who?
Zizi when you know how!

Knock, knock.
Who's there?
Luke.
Luke who?
Luke out, the cops are after you!

Knock, knock.
Who's there?
Genoa.
Genoa who?
Genoa new joke?

Knock, knock.
Who's there?
Emma.
Emma who?
Emma chisit?

Knock, knock.
Who's there?
Plato.
Plato who?
Plato bacon and eggs, please.

Knock, knock.
Who's there?
Heaven.
Heaven who?
Heaven seen you for ages.

Knock, knock.
Who's there?
Boo.
Boo who?
No need to cry, it's only me.

Knock, knock.
Who's there?
Toyota.
Toyota who?
Toyota be a law against knock, knock jokes.

Knock, knock.
Who's there?
Dinah.
Dinah who?
Dinah thirst, can I have a drink of water, please?

Knock, knock.
Who's there?
Police.
Police who?
Police let me in, it's raining.

Knock, knock.
Who's there?
Owen.
Owen who?
Owen will you open this door?

Knock, knock.
Who's there?
Hans.
Hans who?
Hans up who wants a sweet?

Knock, knock.
Who's there?
Vaughan.
Vaughan who?
Vaughan day I'll be grown up.

Knock, knock.
Who's there?
Denial.
Denial who?
Denial's a river in Egypt.

Knock, knock.
Who's there?
Tennis.
Tennis who?
Tennis five plus five.

Knock, knock.
Who's there?
Passion.
Passion who?
Just passion by.

Knock, knock.
Who's there?
Stella.
Stella who?
Stella no answer.

Knock, knock.
Who's there?
Jimmy.
Jimmy who?
Jimmy a kiss.

Knock, knock.
Who's there?
Toodle.
Toodle who?
Bye, bye!

Knock, knock.
Who's there?
Hamish.
Hamish who?
Hamish pocket money do you get?

Knock, knock.
Who's there?
Oswald.
Oswald who?
Oswald my chewing-gum.

Knock, knock.
Who's there?
Oliver.
Oliver who?
Oliver nother chocolate if there are any left.

Knock, knock.
Who's there?
Nadia.
Nadia who?
Nadia head if you can hear me.

Knock, knock.
Who's there?
Mischia.
Mischia who?
Mischia, did you miss me?

Knock, knock.
Who's there?
Lettuce.
Lettuce who?
Lettuce in quick!

Knock, knock.
Who's there?
Jackson.
Jackson who?
Jackson the phone, will you come and speak to him?

Knock, knock.
Who's there?
Esau.
Esau who?
Esau me pulling faces at him, let me in quick!

Knock, knock.
Who's there?
Theresa.
Theresa who?
Theresa big black spider crawling over your foot!

Knock, knock.
Who's there?
Fred.
Fred who?
Fred I can't come out to play today.

Play the Game

Which football team is fat and pink?
Queen's Pork Rangers.

Which football team comes out of an ice-cream cornet?
Aston Vanilla.

Which football team is made up of squirrels?
Nuts Forest.

If you have a referee in football and an umpire in cricket,
what do you have in bowls?
Corn flakes.

Why are batsmen cowards?
Because they're scared of ducks.

Two little boys were having their very first lesson in
playing cricket.
　　'How do you hold the bat?' asked the first.
　　'By the wings,' replied the second.

HAL: Can you skate?
**SAL: I don't know – I can never stand up long
enough to find out.**

What kind of shirts do golfers wear?
Tee shirts.

Where do ghosts play golf?
On a golf corpse.

FIRST GOLFER: I'd move heaven and earth to get a hole in one.
SECOND GOLFER: If I were you I'd concentrate on heaven, you've already moved enough earth.

What did they call the lady wrestler?
The belle of the brawl.

What do swimmers eat off?
A pool table.

Two flies were playing football in a saucer. Said one to the other, 'We'll have to do better than this, we're playing in the cup next week.'

Why was the boxer called Picasso?
He was always on the canvas.

TERRY: My grandad was a boxer.
JERRY: Heavyweight?
TERRY: No, featherweight, he used to tickle his opponents to death.

Young Jim was training to be a boxer, but he wasn't very good at it. Every time he tried to land a punch, he missed. His trainer, who was a kindly man, came up to him and said, 'Keep swinging, lad, the draught might give him a cold.'

What is Transylvania's favourite sport?
Drac racing.

What do Chinese wrestlers have for supper?
Kung food.

MOTHER: Why are you taking the baby's bib out with you, Tommy? I thought you were going to football practice?
TOMMY: Yes, but the coach said we'd be dribbling this week.

Why did the athlete shriek with pain?
He had slipped his discus.

Why did the man with amnesia take up running?
To jog his memory.

What do you get if you cross a camera with a body-builder?
A film that develops itself at the gym.

How did the athlete mend the tear in his shirt?
He ran until he got a stitch.

What did the star receive when it came second in the London Marathon?
A constellation prize.

Did you hear about the two fat men who ran in a race?
One ran in short bursts, the other in burst shorts.

What's the hardest thing about learning to ride a horse?
The ground.

How do you hire a horse?
Stand it on four bricks.

A man went to a riding stables one day and asked if he could hire a horse.

'Certainly, sir,' answered the proprietor. 'How long?'

'The longest you've got,' replied the man. 'Then all my children can ride at the same time.'

JENNY: I went riding this morning.
BENNY: Horseback?
JENNY: Yes, he got home about an hour before me.

Eddie had been riding and came home covered in mud. 'Whatever happened to you?' asked his friend Teddy.

'Well,' said Eddie, 'you know that track through the woods that forks and goes two ways?'

'Yes,' replied Teddy. 'What about it?'

'The horse wanted to go one way and I wanted to go the other.'

'So what did you do?'

'We tossed for it.'

Why did the idiot fisherman cast his line into the air instead of in the water?
He was a fly fisherman.

'And what did you do at the weekend?' his teacher asked little Willy.

'I took my dog fishing, Miss,' replied Willy.

'Did you catch anything?'

'No. Next week I'm going back to using worms.'

Why do people play football?
For kicks.

Why are there ducks in cricket?
Same reason there are fouls in football.

What wears out football boots but has no feet?
The ground.

Which athlete keeps warmest?
The long jumper.

What do athletes eat for lunch?
Runner beans.

What did the world's worst athlete do?
Ran a bath and came in second.

Why is tennis such a noisy game?
Because every player raises a racket.

What's the quietest sport?
Ten-pin bowling – you can hear a pin drop.

MR LARGE: My doctor says I should give up golf.
MR BARGE: He's seen you play too, has he?

HENRY: I love golf. I'd like to go on playing like this for ever.
HARRY: Don't you ever want to get any better?

Jimmy wasn't very good at golf, and as they went round the course he kept asking his companion Jerry for advice. After one particularly disastrous shot he asked, 'How would you have played that one?'
   'In disguise,' replied Jerry.

What goes in pink and comes out blue?
A swimmer in winter.

MRS JONES: I'm going to start swimming regularly. It's one of the best ways of keeping fit and trim.
MRS SMITH: I disagree.
MRS JONES: Why?
MRS SMITH: Have you ever seen a whale?

Did you hear about the idiot who tried to swim the English Channel? When he was a kilometre from the French coast he felt so tired he decided to turn back.

How can a footballer stop his nose running?
Put out a foot and trip it up.

Why can't horses play football?
Because they've got two left feet.

An Honest Crust

Why did the baker work so hard?
To earn an honest crust.

Why else?
He kneaded the dough.

What happened to the grocer who sat on the bacon slicer?
He got a little behind with his work.

How does Jack Frost get to work?
By icicle.

BARRY: Last year I opened a jeweller's shop.
LARRY: Were you successful?
BARRY: No, he called the police.

BOSS: Why are you late for work again?
EMPLOYEE: I overslept.
BOSS: You mean you sleep at home as well?

EMPLOYEE: I'm sorry I'm late. The bus is always late these days.
BOSS: Well, if it's late again tomorrow you'll have to catch an earlier one.

BOSS: You're late. You should have been here at nine o'clock.
EMPLOYEE: Why, what happened?

CLIENT: Right. This is the deal. I give you £1,000 and you do all the worrying for me.
LAWYER: OK. Where's the £1,000?
CLIENT: That's your first worry.

BOSS: Aren't you the same girl who applied for this job a few weeks ago?
GIRL: Yes.
BOSS: And didn't I say I wanted someone older?
GIRL: Yes. That's why I've come back now.

MOLLY: Wasn't your boss angry when you said you'd be leaving next week?
MILLY: Yes. He'd thought I'd meant this week.

HAIRDRESSER: Your hair is going grey, sir.
CUSTOMER: I'm not surprised, the length of time I've been waiting.

BARBER: Were you wearing a red tie when you came in?
CUSTOMER: No.
BARBER: Oh dear, I must have cut your throat.

CUSTOMER: Your hands don't look very clean.
HAIRDRESSER: Sorry, madam, I haven't done a shampoo yet this morning.

BARBER: How do you want your hair cut, young man?
YOUNG JOHNNY: Like Dad's, with a hole on top.

JUDGE: Haven't I seen you before?
MAN IN DOCK: Probably. So many people owe me money I can't remember all their faces.

How did the carpenter break his teeth?
He bit his nails.

What happened to the plumber?
His job went down the drain.

How do vicars make telephone calls?
Parson to parson.

What do you call a vicar on a motorbike?
Rev.

Who delivers mail to footballers?
The goal-post-man.

JANET: Your new boyfriend's a pig farmer, isn't he?
JANE: Yes. How did you know?
JANET: There's a certain air about him.

What happened to the lumberjack who was always late for work?
He was axed to leave.

Why did the baker stop making doughnuts?
He got sick of the hole business.

Why did the other baker give up his job?
The work was so crumby.

What do you give a deaf fisherman?
A herring aid.

Why was the watch salesman bored?
He had too much time on his hands.

Why did the dentist join the army?
So he could become a drill sergeant.

Mr Large (who was as big as his name), thought he was
the only person in the company who could do a proper
day's work. He was fond of boasting proudly, 'It would
take ten men to fill my shoes.'

His secretary, who was tired of hearing this,
mutttered to her colleague, 'They look as if it took ten
cows to make them.'

SECONDHAND CAR SALESMAN: This car is in mint condition, sir.
PROSPECTIVE PURCHASER: So I see, it's got a hole in the middle.

FLYING INSTRUCTOR: Tomorrow you can fly solo.
LEARNER PILOT: How low?

Why was the Chinese chef so tired?
He wokked round the clock.

'Did you hear about the magician who liked to saw people in two? They say he has several half brothers and sisters.'

NAVAL OFFICER: Can you swim?
NEW RECRUIT: Why, can't the navy afford any ships?

Why couldn't the sailors play cards on the ship?
Because the captain was standing on the deck.

LITTLE JOHNNY: When I grow up I want to be a bus driver.
DAD: Well, son, I won't stand in your way.

MR WRINKLY: I'm an antiques collector.
MR SMOOTHY: I know, I've seen your wife.

SAMANTHA: You said the dentist would be painless but he wasn't.
SELINA: Did he hurt you?
SAMANTHA: No, but he screamed when I bit his finger.

Why did the dentist become a brain surgeon?
His drill slipped.

ROB: How's your job at the market garden?
BOB: Problems keep cropping up.

BOSS, INTERVIEWING JOB APPLICANT: We have early hours here. Would that trouble you?
JOB APPLICANT: No, I don't mind how early I leave.

MR WHITE: How's your job as a history lecturer?
MR BLACK: There's no future in it.

GWEN: What's wrong with your boss?
BEN: Nothing a funeral wouldn't cure.

What's another name for a butcher's boy?
A chop assistant.

SUSIE: There's a man at the door with a wooden leg.
DAD: Tell him to hop it.

SALLY: There's a man at the door selling bees.
DAD: Tell him to buzz off.

'Do you like working at the clock factory?'
'Only time will tell.'

'Do you like working at the balloon factory?'
'We can't keep up with inflation.'

'Do you like working at the banana importers?'
'Yes, but I keep slipping up.'

'Do you like working on the new ring road?'
'Yes, but I don't know which way to turn.'

'Do you like working at the funfair?'
'It makes my head spin.'

'Do you like working at the pie factory?'
'No, it didn't pan out.'

A taxi driver discovered some kippers someone had left in the back of his cab, and took them to the lost property office. The attendant told him that if no one had claimed them in six months he could have them.

Why did the secretary put a sticking plaster on her pay cheque?
She got a cut in her salary.

What's an exporter?
A man who used to work on the railways.

Why was the poet broke?
Because rhyme doesn't pay.

What does a trade unionist do if his nose goes on strike?
Picket.

What's an operetta?
A girl who works for British Telecom.

What does one crow phone operator say to the other?
'I have a caw for you.'

What did the rubber band do when it joined the army?
Snapped to attention.

What happened to the sardine fisherman?
He got canned.

What happened when the karate champion joined the army?
The first time he saluted he nearly killed himself.

Why was the idiot sacked from his job at the greengrocer's?
Because he threw away all the bent bananas.

I Never Forget a Face, But . . .

I never forget a face, but in your case I'll make an exception.

ROMEO: Is that perfume I smell?
JULIET: It is and you do.

ROMEO: How long is it possible to live without a brain?
JULIET: I don't know. How old are you?

WALLY: What do you think of my musical talent?
SALLY: I think in your case the song should go 'I've No Business in Show Business'.

LEN: I call my girlfriend Peach.
KEN: Because she's sweet and pretty?
LEN: No, because she has a heart of stone.

BETTY: How do you spell 'nutcase' with just one letter?
HETTY: I don't know.
BETTY: U.

DOREEN: Oh, I love nature.
**MAUREEN: That's very generous of you
considering what nature has done for you!**

ANDY: Molly's so stupid she can't see beyond the end of
her nose.
**MANDY: Yes, but with her nose that's quite a
long way.**

GILLY: Do you think I'm pretty?
BILLY: In a way.
GILLY: What way?
BILLY: As far away as possible.

DONALD: I'm not myself today.
RONALD: I thought there was an improvement.

EDDY: I'm sorry, my mind's wandering.
TEDDY: Don't worry, it's too weak to get very far.

What's the distance between a stupid person's ears?
Next to nothing.

DAWN: Dad's cooking is getting better.
**SHAUN: You mean you can actually eat what he
cooks?**
DAWN: No, but the smoke is now grey instead of black.

MAURICE: I'm so thirsty my tongue's hanging out.
**DORIS: Is that your tongue? I thought it was a
very ugly tie covered in spots!**

KAY: You have to take Alan at face value.
MAY: And with a face like his, that's not much!

NELLIE: Ted's teeth are like the ten commandments.
KELLY: What do you mean?
NELLIE: Nearly all broken.

LYNNE: I'll have you know I have a mind of my own.
GLYN: Only because no one else wants it!

DAVE: You remind me of the Venus de Milo.
MAVE: Really?
DAVE: Yes, beautiful but not all there.

STEVE: Your face should be on the cover of a magazine.
EVE: Vogue, Cosmopolitan?
STEVE: I was thinking more of *Fur and Feather*.

MAGGIE: And he told me my cheeks were like petals.
AGGIE: Bicycle pedals?

BERNIE: Are you trying to make a fool out of me?
ERNIE: No, I believe in letting nature take its course.

BERYL: My husband is good at everything he does.
ERROL: And from what I've seen he usually does nothing.

'I wouldn't say Charlie has a big mouth, but he's the only person I know who can eat a banana sideways.'

'And is she a beautiful actress?'
'Let's just say she has a perfect face for radio.'

SHEILA: I like the simple things in life.
SHELLEY: Like my brother?

MAUD: Your face should be painted in oils.
CLAUD: Why, because I'm so good-looking?
MAUD: No, because you've got a face like a sardine!

MARK: I'm nobody's fool.
CLARK: Perhaps we could find someone to adopt you.

DAISY: I've traced my ancestry back to royalty.
MAISIE: King Kong?

DARREN: I keep talking to myself.
SHARON: I'm not surprised, no one else would listen to you.

DAVE: Did you notice how that singer's voice filled the hall?
MAVE: Yes. And did you notice how many people left to make room for it?

DILYS: I hear Barbara always has to have the last word.
WILLIS: Yes. It wouldn't be so bad if she ever reached it.

DONNA: How's your nose?
DUDLEY: Shut up!
DONNA: So's mine, must be this dry weather.

JAYNE: Sometimes I really like you.
DWAYNE: When's that?
JAYNE: When you're not yourself.

ELLA: Are you getting on well with Eddie?
BELLA: No. He's like a summer cold.
ELLA: What do you mean?
BELLA: I can't get rid of him.

ERIC: See that girl over there? She looks like Helen
Brown.
DEREK: She looks even worse in black!

MRS BADCOOK: It's snowing hard outside. You'd better
stay here for your supper.
**MRS GOODCOOK: The weather doesn't look
that bad to me!**

Two ladies were talking about their student sons who
had just left home to live in their own flats. 'Gerald's
terribly untidy,' said Mrs Black. 'Is your son?'

'Put it this way,' replied Mrs White. 'When the toast
pops up out of his toaster it takes half an hour to find it.'

LIZZIE: I've changed my mind.
LENNY: I thought I'd noticed an improvement.

STARSTRUCK YOUNG GIRL: How can I get to be a great actress and see my name up in lights at the theatre?
HER BROTHER: You could try changing your name to 'Exit'.

NORA: Can you lend me 10p, please? I want to phone a friend.
DORA: Here's 20p. Phone all your friends.

TRACEY: What's your perfume called?
STACEY: 'High Heaven'.
TRACEY: It certainly stinks to it!

MARY: I've just come back from the beauty parlour?
CARY: Pity it was closed.

ANNIE: Did you miss me while I was away?
DANNY: Have you been away?

BERTIE: A funny thing happened to my mother in London.
GERTIE: Really? I thought you were born in Birmingham.

MR HADDOCK: It's so hard to get my wife to eat anything.
MR PADDOCK: Why, is she ill?
MR HADDOCK: No, but she won't stop talking.

FLOYD: Barry had his brain X-rayed.
LLOYD: Really? What did they find?
FLOYD: Nothing.

GARY: My mother thinks I'm a great wit.
LARRY: I'd say she was half right.

GILES: I'm speechless.
MILES: Good. Stay that way.

GLENDA: I have the skin of a newborn baby.
BRENDA: Yes, all red and wrinkled.

JILL: Some people say I'm as pretty as a flower.
JACK: A cauliflower?

JIM: Is it true your brother is a miracle worker?
TIM: Yes, it's always a miracle when he works.

LAURA: I think your brother was built upside down.
NORA: What do you mean?
LAURA: His nose runs and his feet smell.

TEACHER: Can you put this sentence another way: 'He was bent on seeing her.'
CHRISSIE: 'The sight of her doubled him up.'
TEACHER: Not quite, Chrissie. Try another one: 'Her beauty was timeless.'
CHRISSIE: 'Her face would stop a clock.'

GEMMA: I'm one of those people who believe looks aren't everything.
EMMA: In your case they're not anything.

'He has a real chip on his shoulder.'
'It's from the block of wood on his neck.'

'Your son's very full of himself, isn't he?'
'That's because he bites his nails.'

'He bites his nails so much his stomach needs a manicure.'

'There's only one job he'd like – tester in a mattress factory.'

NICK: At least his teeth are all his own.
DICK: You mean he's finished paying for them at last?

MIKE: His right eye must be very interesting.
SPIKE: Why do you say that?
MIKE: Because his left eye looks at it all the time.

Two boys were discussing a friend's girlfriend. 'Do you think she looks bad?' asked Andy.
'She could look worse,' replied Billy, 'if I had better eyesight.'

'Why do they call him Bean?'
'Because the girls string him along.'

'Why do they call him a businessman?'
'Because his nose is always in other people's business.'

'Why do they call him Caesar?'
'Because he's got a lot of gall.'

'Would you say he was bald?'
'Put it this way, you can't look at him in sunlight without wearing dark glasses.'

They're well matched: She's a vegetarian and he's a couch potato.

They're well matched: She's a comedian and he looks funny.

JAMIE: There's no point in telling you a joke with a double meaning.
JENNY: Why not?
JAMIE: You won't get either of them.

CLARRIE: I think faster than you.
HARRY: I know. You've stopped already.

Cindy and Lindy had been having an argument, and Cindy was getting fed up with it. 'Let's come to an agreement,' said Cindy. 'If you promise not to say anything I'll promise not to listen when you do.'

179

MRS WRINKLY: I want to live to be at least 110.
MRS KNOBBLYKNEES: I can see why. Very few people die after that age.

WALLY: My sister lies in the sun for hours and hours.
HOLLY: I expect she wants to be the toast of the town.

Bill and Ben were discussing Lazy Lou. Said Bill, 'The only exercise he takes is watching horror films on the TV.'
  'How is that exercise?' asked Ben.
  'They make his flesh creep,' replied Bill.

Linda was also very lazy. She worked eight hours, and slept eight hours. The trouble was, they were the same eight hours.

Why did Len want to learn how to play the trombone?
It's the only instrument on which you can get anywhere by letting things slide.

'He's so lazy he has his prayers printed and pasted up on the wall and at bedtime says, "Lord, please read them."'

'My brother's so thick that when he went to a mind-reader she only charged him half price.'

JOE: People say I'm one in a million.
FLO: Thank goodness for that.

LAURIE: Lenny was a war baby.
MORRY: I bet. I expect his parents took one look at him and started fighting.

When Lenny was born the doctors took one look at him and slapped his mother.

MRS GREEN: She had a facelift but it didn't work.
MRS BROWN: What happened?
MRS GREEN: The crane broke.

'My brother started at the bottom and liked it so much he's been there ever since.'

LUCY: He's a big gun at work.
LENNY: He should be careful. They might fire him.

'If opportunity knocked he'd probably complain about the noise.'

PAT: I suffer from migraine.
PETE: It's just that your halo's too tight.

NED: Is she good-looking?
**TED: There's a small blemish between her ears –
her face.**

WILL: People say she's like an angel fallen from the sky.
BILL: Pity she landed on her face.

LARRY: Nobody can call him a quitter.
**BARRY: No. He's been fired from every job he's
had.**

SALLY: Is your new boyfriend good-looking?
**SUSIE: He looks much better when I don't wear
my glasses.**

'Anna and Brian make a perfect pair, don't you think?'
'Certainly. She's a pill and he's a headache.'

'Her father is a blacksmith.'
'Is that why she's always forging ahead?'

'Her father is a chimney sweep.'
'Is that why he wears a suit?'

'Her father is a doctor.'
'Boy, can he operate!'

'Her father is an electrician.'
'I'd heard she was well connected.'

'Her father is a vicar.'
'That's why you can't put anything pastor.'

'Her father's an optician.'
'Is that why she makes such a spectacle of herself?'

'He's lucky in one way.'
'What's that?'
'If he went out of his mind no one would know the difference.'

'He flies off the handle a lot.'
'That's because he has a screw loose.'

'He says he can trace his family tree way back.'
'Yes, back to the time he lived in it.'

'He holds people open-mouthed with his sparkling wit.'
'That's because they can't stop yawning.'

'He's good for people's health – when they see him coming they take a long walk.'

'He's the son of a fireman.'
'I'd heard he was going to blazes.'

BILL: I hear Bertie's girl-crazy.
BEN: Yes. None of them will go out with him, that's why he's crazy.

SARAH: A few minutes with Charlie and I feel like jumping for joy.
SUSIE: Do you? I feel like jumping off a cliff!

KATIE: They say Cath's stories always have a happy ending.
CLARA: Well, everyone's happy when they end.

JOHNNY: My sister has lots of men at her feet.
DONNY: What are they, chiropodists?

BRIAN: Is your sister a raving beauty?
RYAN: I'm not sure about the beauty but she's certainly raving!

What's in a Name?

What do you call a man with a plank on his head?
Edward.

What do you call a man with a spade on his head?
Doug.

What do you call a man without a spade on his head?
Douglas.

What do you call a man with a car on his head?
Jack.

What do you call a man with a lavatory on his head?
Lou.

What do you call a woman with two lavatories on her head?
Lulu.

What do you call a woman with a bunch of holly on her head?
Carol.

What do you call a woman with a cat on her head?
Kitty.

What do you call a man with a paper bag on his head?
Russell.

What do you call a man with
a seagull on his head?
Cliff.

What do you call a man with
a crane on his head?
Derek.

What do you call a man with a map on his head?
Miles.

What do you call a man with a car number plate on his
head?
Reg.

What do you call a woman with a radiator on her head?
Anita.

What do you call a man with a wig on his head?
Aaron.

What do you call a man with a mat on his head?
Neil.

What do you call a woman with slates on her head?
Ruth.

What do you call a woman
with a spring on her head?
April.

What do you call a man with a large blue-black mark on his head?
Bruce.

What do you call a man with cat scratches on his head?
Claud.

What do you call a woman with a breeze on her head?
Gail.

What do you call a man with a stamp on his head?
Frank.

What do you call a woman with a twig on her head?
Hazel.

What do you call a man with a boat on his head?
Bob.

What do you call a woman with a tortoise on her head?
Shelley.

What do you call a girl with a tennis racket on her head?
Annette.

What do you call a man with a kilt on his head?
Scott.

What do you call a man with a legal document on his head?
Will.

What do you call a man with a double-decker bus on his head?
Dead!

Into Another World

Why did the boy become an astronaut?
Because he was no earthly good.

What do astronauts wear to keep warm?
Apollo-neck sweaters.

Where do astronauts leave their spaceships?
At parking meteors.

Where do Martians drink beer?
At a Mars bar.

How do you get a baby astronaut to sleep?
You rock-et.

Two astronauts went into a pub on the moon for a drink, but they left after a few minutes. You see, it had no atmosphere.

How do spacemen pass the time on long trips?
They play astronauts and crosses.

Where does Dr Who buy his cheese?
At a dalek-atessen.

Who's tall, dark and a great dancer?
Darth Raver.

Why did Captain Kirk go into the ladies' loo?
To boldly go where no man had gone before.

FIRST SPACEMAN: I'm hungry.
SECOND SPACEMAN: So am I. It must be launch time.

Whose job never lasts very long?
A spaceman's, because as soon as he's hired, he's fired.

What do you call a loony spaceman?
An astronut.

What do you call a space magician?
A flying sorcerer.

LITTLE WILL: I want to be an astronaut when I grow up.
DAD: What high hopes you have.

What does ET stand for?
He's been riding a horse and he finds it painful to sit down.

What do you call an overweight ET?
An extra-cholesterol.

Two aliens from outer space landed on Earth, right in the middle of Manchester. They were fascinated by a set of traffic lights. 'Let's go and talk to her,' said the first alien.

'I saw her first,' replied the second.

'But I'm the one she winked at,' countered the first.

What did the metric alien say?
'Take me to your litre.'

What did the robot say to the petrol pump?
'It's rude to stick your finger in your ear when you're talking to me.'

How does a robot shave?
With a laser blade.

What do you call a robot who always goes the longest way round?
R2 detour.

Do robots have brothers?
No, just tran-sistors.

How do computers make jumpers?
On the interknit.

Why was the computer in pain?
It had a slipped disk.

Why was the computer thin?
It hadn't had many bytes.

Why did the cat sit on the computer?
To keep an eye on the mouse.

What sits in the middle of the world-wide web?
A very, very, large spider.

What's small, expensive, and being constructed at Greenwich?
The millennium gnome.

What holds the moon up?
Moonbeams.

Animal Crackers

How do you feel if you swallow a sheep?
Very baaad.

Where do sheep go for their holidays?
The Baahamas.

TIM: Did you know it takes three sheep to make one jumper?
JIM: I didn't even know sheep could knit!

FIRST SHEEP: Baaa.
SECOND SHEEP: Moo.
FIRST SHEEP: What do you mean, 'moo'?
SECOND SHEEEP: I'm learning a foreign language.

There were so many sheep in the barn they were standing wool to wool.

Why did Bo Peep's sheep call the police?
They'd been fleeced by a crook.

What do you call a cat from the Wild West?
A posse.

What happened to the cat that swallowed a ball of wool?
She had mittens.

MILLY: Why do you call your cat Ben Hur?
TILLY: She was just called Ben until she had kittens.

What's the definition of a caterpillar?
A worm rich enough to buy a fur coat.

What else?
A worm with a sweater on.

How do you tell which end of a worm is the head?
Tickle its middle and see which end smiles.

What did one caterpillar say to the other when they saw a butterfly?
'You'll never get me up in one of those things.'

How does a rabbit keep its fur tidy?
With hare spray.

What do you call a rabbit with fleas?
Bugs Bunny.

What happened to the two rabbits that got married?
They went on a bunnymoon.

Why is a rabbit's nose shiny?
Because its powder puff is at the wrong end.

What does a bald rabbit wear?
A harepiece.

A panda went into a cafe and ordered a hamburger. It sat there quietly for a while, eating the hamburger, then it got up, took out a gun, shot the waiter, and walked out.

'Did you see that?' exclaimed another customer. 'What was it? What happened? What are you doing?' he asked the manager.

The manager was leafing through a book. 'I'm looking it up in the dictionary,' she replied. 'It says: "Panda, eats shoots and leaves".'

What does it mean if you find a horseshoe?
That somewhere a horse is walking around in its socks.

What happens to old horses?
They become nags.

Andy and Mandy were each given a pony for Christmas. The problem was, they had trouble telling them apart.

'Tell you what,' said Andy. 'I'll cut the mane off mine, then we'll know which is which.'

'Fine,' said Mandy. So they cut the mane off one pony, but they still had problems telling them apart.

'Perhaps we could cut the tail of one of them short,' said Mandy. So they trimmed one pony's tail, but they still had trouble telling them apart.

'What are we going to do now?' asked Andy.

'I don't know,' said Mandy. So they sat and thought, and thought and sat.

'Tell you what,' said Mandy, hours later. 'Why don't I have the white one and you have the black one?'

What's a horse's favourite game?
Stable tennis.

What do ducks get if they eat too many chocolates?
Goose pimples.

What do you have when a duck gives you smart answers?
Wise quacks.

DUCK: I got a nose-job from Dr Turkey.
GOOSE: Did it cost a lot?
DUCK: No, it's only a two-dollar bill.

Show me an owl with laryngitis and I'll show you a bird who doesn't give a hoot.

What do you call parrot food?
Polly-filler.

What kind of dog is good at sniffing out young plants?
A bud hound.

How do you stop a dog from digging holes in your garden?
Hide his spade.

196

MUM: Darren, keep that dog out of the house, it's full of fleas!
DARREN: Rover, come away from the house, it's full of fleas!

How did the cat win the milk-drinking competition?
It lapped the field.

Which panto is about a cat in a chemist's shop?
Puss in Boots.

What do bees chew?
Buzzle gum.

HIL: Do you think insects are intelligent?
PHIL: Yes.
HIL: Why?
PHIL: They always manage to work out where we're going to have our picnics.

Where would you put an injured insect?
In an antbulance.

What do you call an insect with an itch?
A jitterbug.

What happened to the hyena who swallowed an Oxo cube?
He made a laughing stock of himself.

What do you call a bear who doesn't wash?
Winnie the Pooh.

Why did the idiot put the chicken in a hot bath?
So she'd lay hard-boiled eggs.

Why *did* the chicken cross the road?
For some fowl reason.

Why did the chicken cross the road halfway?
Because she wanted to lay it on the line.

What has feathers and webbed feet?
A hen wearing scuba gear.

What do you get if you run over a sparrrow with the
lawn-mower?
Shredded tweet.

Why do baby birds leave their nests?
**Wouldn't you leave home if your mother gave you
worms for every meal?**

What made the centipede late for the football match?
Putting his boots on.

What did the boy centipede say to the girl centipede?
'I want to hold your hand, hand, hand . . .'

Which cartoon dog is covered with moisture every
morning?
Scooby Dew.

VISITOR: Why is your dog sitting at my feet and looking up at me like that?
LITTLE JIMMY: Probably because you're eating out of his bowl.

What kind of dogs does a hairdresser keep?
Shampoodles.

MRS SILLY: My cat took first prize in the local bird show.
MRS SOLLY: How come?
MRS SILLY: He ate the prize budgie.

Why did the cat eat the cheese?
So he could sit at the mousehole with baited breath.

'I think when I trod on my cat's paw I hurt his felines.'

SALLY: Our new kitten has a pedigree.
WALLY: You mean you have papers for it?
SALLY: Yes, all over the house.

What do you do with a kangaroo who has appendicitis?
Give him a hoperation.

Did you hear about the exhausted kangaroo?
He was out of bounds.

Why did the mother kangaroo hate wet days?
Because her children couldn't go out to play.

Why did the octopus take his shirt to the laundry?
It was covered with ink spots.

What did the fussy octopus spend all his money on?
Underarm deodorant.

Where does an octopus like to relax?
In an armchair.

Who snatched the baby octopus and held its parents to ransom?
Squidnappers.

How does an octopus go into battle?
Well armed.

How do you get in touch with a fish?
Drop it a line.

Which fish has the lowest voice in the chorus?
The bass.

Which fish can only be seen at night?
A starfish.

What do you call a fish that performs operations?
A sturgeon.

Who's the most powerful fish in the ocean?
The Codfather.

What sea creature is good at maths?
An octoplus.

How do bees make money?
They cell their honey.

What do you call a bee born in May?
A maybe.

What do you call crazy fleas?
Loony ticks.

A man went to the council to complain about his house.
'You see,' he explained, 'me and my brothers all live in
the same two rooms, and they keep animals. One has six
cats, one has four dogs, and one has a pig, and the smell
is terrible.'

'Couldn't you open the windows?' suggested the lady
from the council.

'What, and let all my pigeons escape?' replied the man.

A woman went into a wool shop to buy some wool to
knit her dog a jacket. 'I'm not sure how much I'll need,'
she said, having explained what she wanted the wool for.

'How big is the dog?' asked the assistant.

'I'm not sure,' said the woman.

'Well, bring him in and we'll measure him,' suggested
the assistant.

'Oh, I couldn't do that,' said the woman, 'it's meant to
be a surprise for his birthday.'

DANNY: My dog's got no tail.
ANNIE: How do you know when he's happy?
DANNY: He stops biting me.

ANNIE: My dog's got no nose.
DANNY: How does he smell?
ANNIE: Terrible!

BERTIE: What would you do if you heard a mouse squeak in the night?
GERTIE: I don't know but I wouldn't get up to oil it!

How do you save a mouse that's had a heart attack?
Give it mouse to mouse resuscitation.

A hunter was showing off his trophies to a visitor, who admired his bearskin rug. 'I shot the bear in Canada,' said the hunter. 'I was sorry to kill him but it was him or me.'

'He makes a better rug that you would,' replied the visitor.

What cow is a famous rock singer?
Moodonna.

What cow can speak Russian?
Ma's cow.

What does a Tarzan cow swing on?
A bo-vine.

Why shouldn't you accept a cheque from a kangaroo?
It's likely to bounce.

What was the blessing at the kangaroo wedding?
'May you live hoppily ever after.'

GILL: What's the difference between a kangaroo and a matterbaby?
BILL: What's a matterbaby?
GILL: Nothing, but it's nice of you to ask.

Did you hear the story about the blind skunk?
It fell in love with a drainpipe.

How do you stop a skunk smelling?
Chop off its nose.

What did the skunk say when the wind changed
direction?
'It's all coming back to me now.'

How many skunks does it take to raise a big stink?
A phew.

Mr and Mrs Skunk had a baby called In, and one day In
wandered off on his own and got lost.
　　Mrs Skunk was very upset, and looked everywhere for
him, but she couldn't find him. 'Don't worry, dear,' said
Mr Skunk. 'I'll find him.'
　　So off he went and, sure enough, came home a little
while later accompanied by In.
　　'However did you find him?' asked Mrs Skunk.
　　'Instinct,' replied Mr Skunk.

What did the idiot call his pet tiger?
Spot.

How do monkeys make toast?
Put it under the g'rill-a.

A gorilla went into a cafe and ordered a strawberry milk shake. The waitress was very surprised, but she served the gorilla, and then went to tell the manager.

'Here's our chance to make a bit of money,' thought the manager. So he went to give the gorilla the bill himself.

The gorilla offered him a £10 note, which the manager pocketed without giving any change, thinking the gorilla would know nothing about the value of money. 'We don't get many gorillas in here,' he said, conversationally.

'With milk shakes at £10 a time, I'm not surprised,' replied the gorilla.

What do you call an overweight gorilla?
A chunky monkey.

Why do giraffes have such long necks?
Because their feet smell.

If a giraffe gets its feet wet does it catch a cold?
Yes, but not until the next week.

What's tall, yellow and comes out in spring?
A giraffe-odil.

What do you get if you cross a giraffe with a hedgehog?
A very tall toothbrush.

What did the little hedgehog say when it backed into a
rose bush?
'Is that you, mother?'

What happened when the hedgehog fought the rabbit?
The hedgehog won on points.

What do you call a rabbit hole inspector?
A burrow surveyor.

What do you get if you pour boiling water down a rabbit
hole?
Hot, cross bunnies.

What animal uses a nutcracker?
A toothless squirrel.

What causes a chicken to go red all over?
Henbarrassment.

How do baby hens dance?
Chick to chick.

What did the little chick say to the henhouse bully?
Why don't you peck on someone your own size?

Did you hear about the hen that was fed on sawdust?
**She laid six eggs – five chicks had wooden legs
and the sixth was a woodpecker.**

What do you call a gobbler who thinks he knows
everything?
A smirky turkey.

What happens when ducks fly upside down?
They quack up.

Why do ducks look sad?
**Because when they preen their feathers they get
down in the mouth.**

A man went to an auction sale and started bidding for a
parrot. The bidding went up and up, but finally the man
managed to buy the bird. Then he realized he didn't even
know if it talked, so he asked the auctioneer.

'Of course,' he replied. 'Who do you think was
bidding against you?'

Why was the owl so proud?
He had an entry in Whoo's Whoo.

What owl robs the rich to give to the poor?
Robin Hoot.

Little Jenny was given a kitten, and as she sat stroking it in front of the fire, the kitten started to purr.
'Mum, come quick!' she called. 'The kitten's boiling!'

What's a grasshopper?
An insect on a pogo stick.

How does a flying bug know when it's successful?
When it brings someone to their sneeze.

What did the wasp say to the bluebottle?
'I must fly now, but I'll give you a buzz later.'

What do you call trousers worn by small insects?
Ants' pants.

What insect talks about you behind your back?
A cattypillar.

What's a male insect called in Scotland?
A laddie bug.

Why do spiders taste like chewing-gum?
Because they're wrigglies.

What did the worm journalist work for?
An underground newspaper.

What did the boy maggot say to the girl maggot?
'What's a nice girl like you doing in a joint like this?'

What should you do if someone steals your budgie?
Send for the flying squad.

What kind of cows live in the Arctic?
Eskimoos.

Why do cows lie down in the rain?
To keep each udder warm.

Why did the farmer feed his cows on lottery tickets?
He wanted them to give rich milk.

How do you count a large herd of cows?
With a cowculator.

What happens to cows in hot summers?
They give evaporated milk.

What was the mad calf studying for?
Her BSEs.

What key do cows sing in?
Beef flat.

A city girl was watching a cow chewing its cud and said
to the farmer, 'Doesn't it cost you a lot to buy all your
cows chewing-gum?'

Which animals are good at maths?
Rabbits multiply well but only a snake can be an adder.

BABY SNAKE: Are we poisonous?
MOTHER SNAKE: Why do you ask?
BABY SNAKE: I've just bitten my tongue.

What do you call a neurotic octopus?
A crazy, mixed-up squid.

What do you give a rodent with bad breath?
Mousewash.

What did the baby mouse say when it saw a bat for the first time?
'Mum, come quickly, I've just seen an angel!'

What happened when the dog got laryngitis?
He was totally yelpless.

DOG OWNER: Have you got anything to cure the fleas on my dog?
VET: Maybe – what's wrong with the fleas?

MRS BACK: I entered my dog in the dog show and won first prize.
MRS FRONT: Well done.
MRS BACK: Thank you, but I'd rather the dog had won.

BEN: Why's your dog called Isaiah?
KEN: Because one eye's higher than the other.

A pony owner called out the vet because he couldn't get his pony to move. The vet gave the animal an injection, and it went galloping off.

'That's marvellous!' said the owner. 'How much do I owe you?'

'Ten pounds,' replied the vet.

The owner held out £30. 'Better give me £20 worth of that stuff, otherwise I'll never catch him!'

What do you do with a bee in winter?
Try to swarm it up.

What sport do drones play?
Beesball.

What's even better than a talking dog?
A spelling bee.

What do you call a nosy bee?
A buzzy body.

What bee story did R. L. Stevenson write?
Dr Jekyll and Mr Hive.

What's yellow, orange, black and buzzes?
Carrots and bees.

Why do elephants paint the soles of their feet yellow?
So they can hide upside down in bowls of custard.

Have you ever found an elephant in a bowl of custard?
No.
Shows how good a disguise it is, doesn't it?

Why did the elephant sit on an orange?
He wanted to play squash.

Why don't elephants eat penguins?
They can't get the wrappers of.

Why do elephants wear sandals?
To stop their feet from sinking into the sand.

Why do ostriches bury their heads in the sand?
To see how many elephants aren't wearing sandals.

Is it difficult to bury an elephant?
Yes, it's a huge undertaking.

How do you get an elephant in a matchbox?
Take out the matches first.

Can an elephant jump higher than a tree?
Yes, trees can't jump.

How can you tell if an elephant's been in your bed?
It will be full of peanut shells.

How do you get an elephant in a telephone box?
Open the door.

What's a jumbo jet?
A flying elephant.

Why can't two elephants go swimming at the same time?
They only have one pair of trunks.

What did Mrs Elephant say to Mr Elephant?
**'Darling, we are expecting the thunder of not
very tiny feet.'**

What do you do with a blue elephant?
Try to cheer it up.

What do you do with a green elephant?
Wait until it's ripe.

What do you call an elephant wearing rubber boots?
A wellyphant.

Why wasn't the elephant allowed on the train?
His trunk wouldn't fit in the luggage rack.

Why did the elephant want to be left alone?
Because two elephants is a crowd.

Why are elephants so clever?
They have lots of grey matter.

How do you stop an elephant from charging?
Take away his credit cards.

Where do elephants put their guests?
In the trunk room.

Where do elephants live in Italy?
Tuskany.

What's big and grey and always points north?
A magnetic elephant.

What's big and grey and good at sums?
An elephant with a calculator.

What's worse than being an elephant with hay fever?
Being a centipede with athlete's foot.

What's grey, has wings, and gives money to babies?
The tusk fairy.

What's big, grey and flies?
An elephant in a helicopter.

What's an elephant's least favourite carol?
'The Holly and the Ivory'.

What's big, grey and needs no ironing?
A drip-dry elephant.

An Englishman, a Welshman and a Scotsman were walking through a field when they spotted a cow. The Englishman said, 'Look, there's an English cow.'

The Welshman said, 'No, it's a Welsh cow.'

'You're both wrong,' said the Scotsman. 'It's a Scottish cow – look, it's got bagpipes underneath.'

A mouse walked into a music shop and asked to buy a mouse organ. The owner was amazed. 'In twenty years,' he said, 'no one has asked for a mouse organ, and you're the second in a week.'

'Ah,' said the mouse, 'that must have been our Monica.'

What does a caterpillar do on 1st January?
Turns over a new leaf.

What do you give a constipated canary?
Chirrup of figs.

How can you save money on pet food?
Buy a polar bear – it lives on ice.

A man exploring the jungle came face to face with a lion, and fainted with fear. When he came to, he saw that the lion was down on its knees praying.

'Th-th-thank you for not eating me,' the man stuttered.

'Shh,' said the lion. 'I'm saying grace.'

What are the best steps to take when you meet a lion?
Very big ones!

What's a pelican's favourite fish?
Anything that fits the bill.

Why was the whale a bully?
He liked to pick on shrimps.

What did one dolphin say to the other?
'You did that on porpoise.'

MR GREEN: I want to buy a chicken.
MR BROWN: Do you want a pullet?
MR GREEN: No, I'll carry it home in the car.

Why did the hen sit on the axe?
So she could hatch-et.

BILL: Why do you call your pig Ink?
BEN: He's always running out of the pen.

What kind of petrol does a tortoise use?
Shell.

Why did the dog run into the corner when the doorbell rang?
He was a boxer.

PROSPECTIVE PURCHASER: This dog's legs are too short.
PET SHOP OWNER: But they do all reach the floor, sir.

What animal do you look like when you have a bath?
A little bear.

What's white, furry and smells of peppermint?
A polo bear.

What did the bookworm say to the librarian?
'May I burrow this book?'

What happened when the turkey got into fight?
He had the stuffing knocked out of him.

What's a pig's laundry called?
Hogwash.

What do you call a blind deer?
No-eye deer.

What kind of birds go to church?
Birds of prey.

Where do pigs like to sit?
On pork benches.

Two fish were swimming in a river when it began to rain. 'Quick,' said one, 'let's go and shelter under that bridge.'

What kind of sandals do frogs wear?
Open-toad.

What do you call a frog spy?
A croak and dagger agent.

What's a frog's favourite drink?
Croaka-cola.

What did the frog do when it joined the army?
Hopped to it.

What happens if a frog parks on a double yellow line?
He gets toad away.

Why was 1996 a good year for frogs?
It was a leap year.

A man bought a mousetrap and then discovered he had
no cheese with which to bait it, so he painted a picture
of some cheese and put it in the trap. When he checked
it next morning he discovered the picture of the cheese
had gone and in its place was a picture of a mouse.

What's the difference between a buffalo and a bison?
You can't wash your hands in a buffalo.

Did you hear the story about the peacock?
It's a beautiful tail.

WAYNE: I used to think I was a dog but the doctor cured me.
JAYNE: You're all right now, are you?
WAYNE: Never better. Here, feel my nose.

Why is it impossible to play a trick on a snake?
Because you can't pull its leg.

What happens when a frog's car breaks down on a motorway?
It gets toad away.

'Look at the speed of that!' said one bird to another as a jet flew overhead.
His friend was unimpressed. 'You'd fly that fast if your tail was on fire'.

Lucky Dip

How do you find a needle in a haystack?
Walk on it in your bare feet.

How do snowmen fasten things together?
With igloo.

Who wrote *Great Eggspectations*?
Charles Chickens.

What did all the king's horses and all the king's men say
when Humpty Dumpty fell off the wall?
'Scrambled eggs for breakfast again, chaps.'

BERYL: Do you like my shawl? It's 100 years old.
CHERYL: Did you make it yourself?

TEACHER: If you had five ice-creams and your friend
asked for one how many would you have left?
GREEDY GERTIE: Five.

How do they make sugar cubes?
From square sugar beet.

LADY LOTTADOSH, TO NEW CHAUFFEUR: What's your name, my man?
CHAUFFEUR: James, m'lady.
LADY LOTTADOSH: I usually call my chauffeurs by their surnames, James. What is yours?
CHAUFFEUR: Darling, m'lady.
LADY LOTTADOSH: Drive on, James.

Why did the man keep his wife under the bed?
He thought she was a little potty.

What runs around all day and spends the night with its tongue hanging out?
A training shoe.

What's the best way to make a pair of trousers last?
Make the jacket first.

FRED: Have you heard the joke about the dirty shirt?
TED: No.
FRED: That's one on you.

Mrs Broadbeam was looking at clothes in a shop when the assistant came up to help her. 'I'm looking for a dress to wear around the house,' explained Mrs Broadbeam.

The assistant looked worried. 'I'm afraid we haven't got any that big,' she said.

MR BROADBEAM: I'd like a shirt to match my eyes, please.
ASSISTANT: I'm afraid we don't sell bloodshot shirts, sir.

HARRY: That's a nice Easter tie.
LARRY: Why do you call it an Easter tie?
HARRY: Because it's got egg all over it.

MISS TRIMHIPS: May I try on that bikini in the window, please?
ASSISTANT: No, madam, you'll have to use the changing-room like everyone else.

What kind of hat has fingerprints?
A felt one.

MILLY: Whenever I'm down in the dumps I buy a new hat.
TILLY: I always wondered where you bought them.

LADY LOTTADOSH: Perkins, I saw a mouse in the west wing.
PERKINS: Very good, m'lady, I'll ascertain if the cat is available to dine.

What did the sea say to the shore?
Nothing, it just waved.

Why doesn't the sea fall over the horizon?
It's tied.

What did the carpet say to the desk?
'I can see your drawers.'

What do you call a press photographer?
A flash guy.

What are everyone's favourite orders?
Postal orders.

LITTLE JOHNNY: What's that book the people in the orchestra keep looking at?
DAD: That's the score.
LITTLE JOHNNY: Really? Who's winning?

Who lives in a paper bag and hangs around a French cathedral?
The lunchpack of Notre Dame.

JIM: What made you decide to take up parachuting?
TIM: A plane with two failed engines.

What did the daft woman say when she saw her son in the cadet parade?
'Oh, look, our Harry's the only one in step.'

What's a paratrooper?
An army dropout.

222

SALLY: Do you think this is a good photo of me?
SUSIE: It makes you look older.
SALLY: Oh good, it'll save me having one taken next year.

MR QUIET: Didn't you hear me banging on your ceiling last night?
MR NOISY: That's all right, we had a party and were making quite a lot of noise ourselves.

JOHN: You've just written a cheque for £1,000.
DON: It's a present for my girlfriend.
JOHN: But you haven't signed it.
DON: I know. I'm sending it anonymously.

MAN ON PHONE: Will you marry me?
GIRL ANSWERING PHONE: Of course. Who's calling?

SHARON: Why did they put you in prison if you were making big money?
DARREN: Because I made it 5mm too big.

A prison warder was escorting a prisoner when his hat blew off. Said the prisoner, 'I'll get it for you.'

'I'm not daft,' said the warder. 'You stay here and I'll get it.'

What did the crook who stole a calendar get?
Twelve months.

Why was the musician arrested?
He got into treble.

Which film star suffers from indigestion?
Burp Reynolds.

What did the idiot have at the top of his ladder?
A sign saying Stop!

How do you make an idiot laugh on Friday afternoon?
Tell him a joke on Monday morning.

What's the difference between a peeping tom and
someone who's just got out of the bath?
One's rude and nosey; the other's nude and rosy.

TRACEY: Have you seen that statue called 'The Thinker'?
STACEY: Yes. I wonder what he's thinking about?
TRACEY: I expect he's wondering how to get home
without any clothes on.

How do you tell the sex of a chromosome?
Take its genes off.

Which nursery rhyme character lives with her granny
and tells naughty jokes?
Little Rude Riding Hood.

Which French town has two lavatories in each house?
Toulouse.

What do boys with spots have in common with non-slip rugs?
They both have pimples on their bottoms.

A man at the cinema went out in the interval to buy an ice-cream. When he returned he asked the lady at the end of the row, 'Did I tread on your foot a few moments ago?'

'Yes,' she said, looking cross.

'Oh good,' said the man, 'I wasn't sure if this was my row.'

One lovely summer's day the village of Wittering Parva was holding its annual fete. Lady Primm was having tea on the vicarage lawn with the vicar and his wife, and the vicar's cat strolled up, sat down, and began to wash the middle of its back. 'I wish I was agile enough to do that, don't you?' asked Lady Primm.

The vicar looked down at the cat, which was by now washing its bottom!

Mandy was telling her friends about the lovely new flat she'd moved into. 'It's marvellous,' she said. 'I can lie in bed and watch the sun rise.'

'So what,' replied her friend Milly. 'I can sit on a chair and watch the kitchen sink.'

DENTIST: What kind of filling shall I put in your tooth?
PATIENT: Chocolate cream, please.

What happened when the 24-stone man climbed into the lions' pen at the zoo?
He ate two of them before they could get him out.

'What's the weather like?'
'I don't know, it's too foggy to see.'

DAD: Would you like a pocket calculator for your birthday?
DEAN: No thanks, I know how many pockets I've got.

JOE: Why don't you play cards with John any more?
MO: Would you play cards with someone who cheats?
JOE: No.
MO: Neither will John.

A farmer was showing the school swot round his farm. In one big field there were lots of sheep.

'How many sheep do you think there are?' asked the farmer.

'Four hundred and twenty-three,' replied the boy.

'That's very clever of you,' said the farmer, impressed. 'You're just right. How did you count them so quickly?'

'Oh, it was very easy,' said the boy. 'I just counted all the legs and divided by four.'

BENNY: Did you hear about the group of amateur musicians who played Beethoven in the village hall?
JENNY: No, what happened?
BENNY: Beethoven lost.

What do you need to play the harp?
A lot of pluck.

FARMER GILES: I can't decide whether to buy a bicycle or a cow for the farm.
FARMER MILES: You'd look silly riding a cow.
FARMER GILES: I'd look even sillier trying to milk a bicycle.

How do you keep flies out of the kitchen?
Put a bucket of manure in the dining-room.

ROMEO: What do you want for your birthday?
JULIET: I'd like a surprise.
ROMEO: OK – boo!

What was the famous cat composer called?
Pussini.

FIRST PENSIONER: How's your new hearing-aid? Can you hear better now?
SECOND PENSIONER: Yes, next Wednesday.

What's the definition of a bathing beauty?
A girl worth wading for.

What's red and lies upside down at the side of the road?
A dead bus.

Why did the bed spread?
Because it saw the pillow slip.

Did you hear the story of the peacock who played football?
It was a beautiful tail.

DAFT DORA: A packet of birdseed, please.
PET SHOP OWNER: What kind of birds have you got?
DAFT DORA: I haven't got any yet, I want to grow some.

What was the locksmith doing in the middle of the night when the police spotted him at the jeweller's?
Making a bolt for the door.

What has four wheels and flies?
A dustcart.

Little Laura was on an outing with the Brownies. They were walking through a field of cows when her beret blew off. It was some time before the group leader realized she was no longer with them, and she went back to look for Laura.

228

'What's happened? Are you all right?' asked the Brownie leader.

'Yes, thank you,' replied Laura. 'It's just that my beret blew off and I had to try on six before I found it.'

Dean took Jean to the cinema. 'Can you see all right?' he asked.

'Yes, thank you,' she replied.

'No one is blocking your view?'

'No.'

'And your seat is comfortable?'

'Oh, yes, very comfortable, thank you.'

'In that case,' said Dean, 'would you mind swapping places with me?'

CINEMA BOX OFFICE ATTENDANT: That's the sixth ticket you've bought.
CINEMAGOER: I know, but there's a girl in there who keeps tearing them up.

JAN: Ooh, that film sent shivers down my spine!
JOHN: So that's what happened to my ice-cream.

What's brown, hairy and wears sunglasses?
A coconut in disguise.

NICK: What does 'coincidence' mean?
FLIC: Funny, I was just going to ask you that.

Which famous detective takes bubble baths?
Sherlock Foams.

DEL: I'm going to get up at dawn tomorrow to watch the sun rise.
TEL: If you'd picked a better time I'd have come with you.

BEN: What time did your clock stop?
KEN: I don't know, I was out.

What did one candle say to the other?
'You're getting on my wick.'

Who eats spinach and makes clothes?
Popeye the tailor-man.

OLD TRAMP: Give us £5 for a cup of coffee, guv.
PASSER-BY: A cup of coffee doesn't cost £5!
OLD TRAMP: No, but I'm expecting company.

'I hear the police are looking for a man with one eye called Jack Robinson.'
'What's his other eye called?'

Sammy was in hospital recovering from an operation when his friend Tammy arrived to see him.
    'I've brought you a present – your favourite chocolates,' said Tammy.
    'But the box is half empty,' said Sammy, looking at it.
    'Yes, well, they're my favourites, too,' replied Tammy.

Can February march?
No, but April may.

A little girl was struggling to reach a doorbell so a kindly lady passing by offered to help her. The lady reached up and rang the bell.

'Thank you,' said the little girl. 'Now we'd better both run for it!'

A teacher was trying to impress upon her class the importance of honesty. 'If you found some money,' she asked one boy. 'Would you keep it?'

'Oh, no, Miss,' replied Darryl.

'Good,' said his teacher. 'What would you do with it?'

'I'd spend it,' replied Darryl.

HARRY: I dream of cricket every night.
LARRY: Don't you ever dream of girls?
HARRY: What, and miss my innings?

A motorist driving the wrong way down a one-way street was stopped by a policeman. 'Do you know where you're going, sir?' he asked

'Yes,' replied the motorist. 'But I must be late, everyone else is coming back.'

POLICEMAN: You were driving at 80 miles per hour, Miss.
YOUNG DRIVER: **Isn't that marvellous? I only passed my test yesterday!**

DAD: Can you just check that my indicators are working?
SON: **Yes, no, yes, no, yes, no.**

A piece of string walked into a bar and ordered a glass of beer.

'I'm sorry,' said the barman. 'But we don't serve pieces of string.'

Then a second piece of string walked in and ordered a glass of cider.

'I'm sorry,' said the barman. 'We don't serve pieces of string.'

A third piece of string, who had been watching what was going on, tied a knot in one end of itself before walking into the same bar and ordering a glass of lager.

'You're another piece of string. We don't serve pieces of string in here,' said the barman. 'Didn't you hear what I said to the others?'

'No, I'm frayed knot,' replied the third piece of string.

Why did the Joneses call both their sons Edward?
Because two Eds are better than one.

What's a gossip?
Someone who lets the chat out of the bag.

232

Why do you feel cold when you lose your two front teeth?
No central 'eating.

JUDGE: Do you plead guilty or not guilty?
PRISONER IN DOCK: Do I have any other choices?

JUDGE: This is the tenth time you've been up before me. Fined £500.
PRISONER: As you've fined me nine times before, don't I qualify for a discount?

JUDGE: This man's wallet was in the inside pocket of his jacket. How did you manage to remove it?
PRISONER: I usually charge people £25 a time for that kind of information.

Why was the man sent to prison for something he didn't do?
He didn't jump into the getaway car fast enough.

What smells terrible but is useful to the army?
A septic tank.

Did you hear about the man who jumped into a cesspit?
He committed sewercide.

What does CID stand for?
Coppers in disguise.

How do you make a cigarette lighter?
Take out the tobacco.

Harry, who was the world's worst driver, took his friend Larry on a motoring holiday in the Alps. Every time they went round the hairpin bends, with tyres screeching, Larry was terrified. He tried to hide his fear, but eventually Harry realized his friend was scared.

'Don't worry,' he said cheerfully. 'Do what I do on these bends – close your eyes.'

Which part of a car is the laziest?
The wheels, they're always tyred.

What car does a rich comedian drive?
A droll's Royce.

Why do large cars go quickly?
They have a big boot behind.

What's the best thing to take if you're run down?
The number of the car that hit you.

MRS JOLLY: What is your son going to be by the time he has passed all his exams and left school?
MRS JELLY: An old-age pensioner.

MR JELLY: When I go to the corner shop the shopkeeper always shakes my hand.
MR JOLLY: I expect it's to make sure it stays out of his till.

How can you help a starving cannibal?
Give him a hand.

Did you hear about the cannibal who went on a sea voyage?
    At dinner on the first night he ignored the menu and asked to see the passenger list.

FIRST CANNIBAL: We had burglars yesterday.
SECOND CANNIBAL: Did you enjoy them?
FIRST CANNIBAL: Yes, but they weren't as good as missionaries.

What do you serve, but never eat?
A tennis ball.

What happens if you wrap your sandwiches in your favourite comic?
You get crumby jokes.

What crisps fly?
Plain ones.

What did the tree say to the axe?
'I'm stumped.'

BOATING LAKE ATTENDANT: Come in, number 9, your time's up.
HIS ASSISTANT: We've only got eight boats.
BOATING LAKE ATTENDANT: Oh dear, are you in trouble, number 6?

Dopey Donald walked into a bank and asked, 'Who dropped a wad of money wrapped in an elastic band?'
All the customers replied, 'I did.'
'Well,' said Donald, 'here's the elastic band.'

How can you make your money grow?
Look at it through a magnifying glass.

SUSIE: I got an anonymous letter today.
SALLY: Really? Who was it from?

DOCTOR: How did you burn both your ears?
IDIOT: I was doing the ironing when the phone rang and I picked up the iron by mistake.
DOCTOR: But you've burnt *both* ears.
IDIOT: Yes, as soon as I'd put the phone down it rang again.

When does a man become two men?
When he's beside himself.

BEN: Did you hear the joke about the rope?
LEN: No, what about it?
BEN: Oh, skip it.

NELLY: Do you have trouble making up your mind?
KELLY: Well, yes and no.

How do you make a fishing-net?
You start with a lot of holes and join them together.

What's the best way to save money?
Forget who you borrowed it from.

JANE: Is your brother very conservation-minded?
WAYNE: Well, he likes to save on soap and water.

ANNE: What are you wearing for the fancy dress party?
DAN: Two shirts, two pairs of trousers, two jackets and four socks.
ANNE: What are you going as?
DAN: Twins.

What do you need to play the piano?
A bunch of keys.

Did you hear about the man who burgled a farm?
He was caught when the pig squealed.

The circus owner was chatting to the clown about old times. 'Do you remember that chap who used to put his arm in the lion's mouth? What was his name?'

'I don't remember,' replied the clown, 'but I've heard they call him Lefty now.'

What happened to the man who stole the milk tanker?
He was taken into custard-y.

What kind of TV programme is soothing to watch?
A sit-calm.

STICKER ON AN OIL TANKER: We fuel all of the people all of the time.

What kind of ship is full of rabbits?
A harecraft carrier.

Who is king of the rock garden?
Elvis Parsley.

MR WOOD: My wife kept saying she wanted a Jaguar so I bought her one.
MR WOODEN'T: What happened?
MR WOOD: It bit off her arm.

A mean man went to a saddler's and asked for one spur.

'Don't you want a pair?' asked the saddler.

'No,' replied the man. 'If I can get one side of the horse to go the other is sure to go with it.'

FIRST FARMER: Is that scarecrow of yours any good?
SECOND FARMER: It certainly is. The crows are so frightened of it they're bringing back the seeds they took last week.

DEAN: Why did you throw away your alarm clock?
JEAN: It kept ringing while I was asleep.

When can't you get money from an egg?
When it's broke.

LYNN: Remember when I was broke and you lent me some money and I said I'd never forget you?
FLYNN: Yes.
LYNN: Well, I'm broke again.

Why does it cost a lot to have floor covering fitted?
Carpet tax.

Why was the policeman sad?
He couldn't take his panda to bed with him.

What did the policeman call out to the speeding
sweater?
'Oi, you, pull over.'

What coughs and fires bullets?
A sick shooter.

When are eyes not eyes?
When the wind makes them water.

Where does a mermaid sleep?
On a water bed.

Why was the cowboy called Paleface?
Because he had a face like a bucket.

SHERIFF: Which way did the computer programmer go?
COWBOY: Data way!

Have you heard the definition of the word 'bath'?
**It's a magic word that makes dogs and little boys
vanish.**

Did you hear about the man who bought a paper shop?
It blew away.

Why did the idiot plant pennies?
He wanted to raise some cash.

Where do fools shop?
Insanesbury's.

DARREN: So far today I've only made one mistake.
SHARON: What was that?
DARREN: I got out of bed.

MRS WIDE: I'm going Christmas shopping, but I'm dreading the crowds.
MRS LARGE: Yes, they're full of brotherly shove.

MACK: I wish you'd only sing Christmas carols.
JACK: Why?
MACK: Then I'd only have to listen to you once a year.

Why is a forger a good person?
Because he's always writing wrongs.

Why did the idiot sleep under his car?
He wanted to get up oily in the morning.

What's full of holes yet strong as iron?
A chain.

What's another name for two policemen on the beat?
A pair of nickers.

What do you get if you pull your knickers up to your chin?
A chest of drawers.

Did you hear about the idiot who had a brain transplant?
The brain rejected him.

What did the idiot do when he found a flea in his ear?
Shot it.

What happened to the fool who wanted to listen to the match?
He singed his ear.

MUM: Will you answer the phone, please?
DAFT DEREK: I can't, I didn't hear its question.

Three identical men went into a car wash. How could you tell which one was the idiot?
He was the one on the bicycle.

Why did the idiot invest in feathers?
He'd heard the stock market was going down.

BILLY: How did you like the film?
GILLY: It was so bad I found it hard to sit through it a second time.

What kind of tree can't you climb?
A lava-tree.

Why did the man scream with pain when he walked into the bar?
It was an iron bar.

What's Welsh for a bypass?
A dai-version.

Why was the boy scout dizzy?
He'd spent the whole day doing good turns.

How can you tell the age of a telephone?
Count its rings.

DILLY: Tell me some more gossip about Jim.
MILLY: I can't. I've already told you more than I've heard myself.

MRS STICK: Our house is so damp the mousetraps catch fish.
MRS STACK: Our house is so rotten it only keeps standing because the woodworm hold hands.

JOHN: Is your new house very big?
DON: No. In fact, it's so small we had to take the wallpaper off to get the furniture in.

What do sad fir trees do?
Pine a lot.

Why did Nelson wear a three-cornered hat?
To keep his three-cornered head warm.

What was Nelson's younger brother called?
Half Nelson.

Did you hear about the man who plugged his electric blanket into the toaster by mistake?
He spent all night popping out of bed.

Why are a monster's hands never more than 11 inches long?
Because if they were 12 inches long they'd be a foot.

Where do you find a Greek's temple?
On the side of his forehead.

What's the difference between a clothes brush and an iceberg?
One brushes coats; the other crushes boats.

Where's spaghetti junction?
Just pasta Birmingham.

Did you hear about the three holes in the ground?
Well, well, well.

SCOUT LEADER: Who can tell me how to start a fire with two sticks?
SMART SCOUT: Make sure one of them's a match.

GAMEKEEPER: Can't you read? That sign says 'No fishing'.
LITTLE BOY: I'm not fishing. I'm giving my pet maggot a bath.

PASSERBY: Did you catch that fish all on your own?
LITTLE BOY: No, a little worm helped me.

NEW FISHERMAN: Is this river good for fish?
EXPERIENCED FISHERMAN: It seems to be, I've never persuaded any to leave it.

KEITH: Did you hear that Ken was arrested for flat feet?
KEVIN: How come?
KEITH: His feet were in the wrong flat.

Which of Robin Hood's men carved things out of wood?
Whittle John.

What did Robin Hood wear to go out for the evening?
A bow tie.

What did one doorknob say to the other?
'It's your turn.'

What's another name for a smile?
A face-lift.

DAD: How did the greenhouse window get broken?
JIMMY: My catapult went off while I was cleaning it.

What's the definition of a chair?
Headquarters for hindquarters.

What can fly underwater?
A wasp in a submarine.

What happens if you don't pay the exorcist's bill?
You get repossessed.

JACK: Every night I dream I'm flying.
JILL: Why don't you sleep on your back?
JACK: I can't fly upside down.

Why did Eric Cantona play football?
For kicks.

Who's the biggest gangster in the sea?
Al Caprawn.

Why do toadstools grow close together?
They don't need mushroom.

Which muppet is always shrouded in fog?
Mist Piggy.

'I wouldn't say he was a gossip, but he gets a sunburned tongue in summer.'

What's purple, round and floats in space?
The planet of the grapes.

TRACEY: Do you believe in free speech?
STACEY: Of course.
TRACEY: In that case may I use your phone?

ALAN: What's the difference between a lavatory and a washbasin?
ANNABEL: I don't know.
ALAN: Then you're not going to use our bathroom!

DENNIS: I've got a dirty magazine.
DIANE: Full of rude pictures?
DENNIS: No, I dropped it in some dog dirt.

Where do you weigh a whale?
At a whale-weigh station.

What happens if you go to sleep with your head under the pillow?
The fairies take out all your teeth!

Alan, Bertie and Chris had a row. 'You're so stupid, Alan,' said Bertie.
    'That's not very nice,' said Chris. 'Say you're sorry.'
    'All right,' said Bertie. 'I'm sorry you're so stupid, Alan.'

TOURIST: Where's the park?
LOCAL: There's no park round here.
TOURIST: But the sign says, 'Park here'.

'Our office is so small we have to drink condensed milk in our coffee.'

Why was the house feeling ill?
It had window panes.

How can you make a thin person fat?
Push him off a cliff and he'll come down plump.

SALESMAN: This hat fits you nicely, sir.
CUSTOMER: But what happens when my ears get tired?

What sort of hat plays cricket?
A bowler.

Which house weighs the least?
A lighthouse.

If a red house is red, and a white house is white, what colour is a greenhouse?
It's no colour, it's made of glass.

ESTATE AGENT: This house hasn't a flaw.
PROSPECTIVE BUYER: What do you walk on then?

JIM: How far is your house from the station?
TIM: Ten minutes' walk if you run.

CHARLIE: How do you do?
CHRISSIE: Do what?
CHARLIE: I mean, how do you feel?
CHRISSIE: With my fingers, of course.
CHARLIE: How do you find yourself?
CHRISSIE: I'm not lost.

Two boys were playing football. Said one, 'Let's go home. It's getting dark and we haven't managed to hit the goal once.'

  'Let's miss it a few more times before we go,' answered the other.

JACK: How do you keep a fool in suspense?
ZACK: I don't know.
JACK: Tell you next week.

What's the definition of ice?
Skid stuff.

Why did the invisible man look in the mirror?
To see if he still wasn't there.

How does an intruder get into the house?
Intruder window.

GILLY: Can you stand on your head?
BILLY: No, it's too high up.

MUM: Have you thought of a hobby you'd like?
LITTLE DAISY: Yes. I'm going to collect worms.
MUM: And what will you do with them when you've got them?
LITTLE DAISY: Press them.

Which rock group do you find in an alley?
The Bowling Stones.

When can your pocket be empty yet have something in it?
When it has a hole in it.

Why did the car have a puncture?
There was a fork in the road.

HARRY: Hollow.
LARRY: What's hollow?
HARRY: An empty greeting.

A family had a holiday on a farm and enjoyed it very much apart from the smell of the pigs. The following year they wanted to go again so they wrote to the farmer asking if he'd still got the pigs. In his reply he wrote, 'We've had no pigs on the farm since you were here last year.'

Did you hear about the farmyard impressionist?
He did the smells.

WINNIE: How's your insomnia?
GINNIE: Awful. Now I can't even get to sleep when it's time to get up.

What did the jack say to the car?
'Let me give you a lift.'

Does your garden have a swing?
No, but it has a beet.

Which Italian secret society beats people up with shopping baskets?
The Raffia.

CUSTOMER: Do you sell invisible ink?
SALESMAN: Certainly, sir. What colour would you like?

How do you start a jelly race?
'Get set.'

What sits in a pushchair wobbling?
A jelly baby.

What do jelly babies wear on their feet?
Gum boots.

WANDA: I heard a new joke. Did I tell it to you?
WILLIE: Is it funny?
WANDA: Yes.
WILLIE: Then you didn't.

A young man walked into a shop and asked for some tight jeans. 'Certainly, sir,' said the shop assistant. 'Walk this way.'

'If they're as tight as yours I'll probably have to,' muttered the young man.

A man walked into a shop carrying a rabbit under his arm. 'Where did you get that pig?' asked the shopkeeper.

'It's not a pig, it's a rabbit,' said the man.

'Shut up,' said the shopkeeper. 'I wasn't talking to you, I was talking to the rabbit.'

How can you jump over three men sitting down?
Play draughts.

What made the kettle sore?
Boils.

252

What happened when a tap, a dog and a tomato ran a race?
The tap was running, the dog took the lead and the tomato tried to ketchup.

What's a maniokleptic?
Someone who walks backwards into shops and leaves things behind.

JENNY: I once bought a paper dress.
JANEY: What was it like?
JENNY: Tearable.

How can you knit a barbed wire fence?
With steel wool.

What do you call a judge with no fingers?
Justice Thumbs.

The judge was only five feet tall – a small thing sent to try us.

JUDGE: Have you ever stolen before?
PRISONER IN DOCK: Now and then.
JUDGE: Where from?
PRISONER: Here and there.
JUDGE: Lock him up.
PRISONER: When do I get out?
JUDGE: Sooner or later.

Little Johnny had been to the circus and his dad was asking him if he'd enjoyed it.

'Oh, yes,' said Johnny. 'But that knife-thrower wasn't much good.'

'Why not?' asked his dad.

'He kept throwing knives at that silly girl and he didn't hit her once.'

What do you call a bald teddy?
Fred bear.

What kind of leather makes the best shoes?
I don't know, but a couple of banana skins make the best slippers.

What has 50 legs but can't walk?
Half a centipede.

GERRY: What are you doing?
TERRY: Writing a letter to myself.
GERRY: What does it say?
TERRY: I shan't know until I get it tomorrow.

An actor went to a theatrical agent. 'What can you do?' asked the agent.

'I do bird impressions,' replied the actor.

'You mean you whistle?' asked the agent.

'No,' said the actor. 'I eat worms.'

Why does a young lady need the letter Y?
Without it she'd be a young lad.

How do you get rid of varnish?
Take away the letter R.

Why should you never put the letter M in the fridge?
It turns ice into mice.

Why does Lucy like the letter K?
It makes Lucy lucky.

What makes cream scream?
The letter S.

Which two letters have nothing between them?
N and P – O is between them.

Which letter is like a vegetable?
P.

What has a bottom at its top?
A leg.

What did the policeman say to his tummy?
You're under a vest.

What's the difference between a nail and a boxer?
One is knocked in; the other knocked out.

MRS FEATHER: I finally stopped Freddie biting his nails.
MRS FLUFF: How did you do that?
MRS FEATHER: I bought him some shoes.

What do rocks eat at teatime?
Marble cake.

MIKE: What do you do when the world is all grey and gloomy?
SPIKE: I deliver newspapers.

What musical instrument never tells the truth?
A lyre.

What has eight feet and sings?
A quartet.

LAURIE: Why do you always play the same piece of music?
LENNIE: Because it haunts me.
LAURIE: That's because you murdered it months ago.

Why did the seaweed blush?
Because it saw the ship's bottom.

How do you know when you're getting old?
The cake costs less than the candles.

Did you hear about the idiot who heard the price of newspapers was going up tomorrow?
He bought all the copies he could find today.

What happens if you keep your nose to the grindstone?
You get a flat face.

Why did the ocean roar?
Because it had lobsters in its bed.

What does one good turn give you?
Most of the duvet.

Did you hear about the man who had problems with his contact lenses?
He couldn't get them on over his glasses.

What occurs once in a minute, twice in every moment but never in a thousand years?
The letter M.

TRAFFIC WARDEN: Why did you park your car where you did?
MOTORIST: Because the notice said, 'Fine for parking'.

'This machine does the work of a dozen men. It almost has a brain.'
'Not if it does that much work it doesn't.'

The foreman on a building site noticed a group of workers, two of which were working while the other just stood still. 'What are you doing?' he asked the non-worker.

'I'm a lamp-post,' replied the man.

'You're fired,' said the foreman.

The man walked off, followed by the other two.

'Not you,' said the foreman. 'Come back.'

'But we can't work in the dark,' said the two men.

MUM: Why are you crying?

BEN: Because Bill's lost his football.

MUM: So why are *you* crying?

BEN: I was playing with it when he lost it.

DILBERT: How much money do you have in your wallet?

DELIA: Between £80 and £90.

DILBERT: That's a lot of money.

DELIA: Not really, £10 isn't that much.

What does a Frenchman have for breakfast?

Huit-heure-bix.

Why did the footballer call his dog Carpenter?

He was always doing little jobs around the house.

What's big, bright and stupid?

A fool moon.

How can you make more of your money?
Fold it up – you'll find it in creases.

What goes farther the slower it goes?
Money.

There were once eight idiots, Doh, Re, Fah, Soh, Lah, and Ti . . .
What about Mi?
Oh, sorry, I forgot about you.

A woman kept going into a shop and buying mothballs. 'You must have lots of moths,' said the shop assistant.
'I have,' agreed the woman. 'And I spend all day throwing mothballs at them but I never seem to hit any.'

A motorist arrested for speeding went to court. 'How did you get on?' asked his friend.
'Fine,' replied the motorist.

Why is money called dough?
Because we all knead it.

A removal man was struggling to move a large wardrobe. 'Why don't you get the other man to help you?' asked the householder.
'He's inside carrying the clothes,' he replied.

'A mousetrap, please, and please hurry, I have to catch a train.'
'We haven't got any that big, sir.'

SHOP ASSISTANT: Haven't I seen you before?
FILM STAR: Perhaps at the movies?
SHOP ASSISTANT: Could be. Where do you usually sit?

Why don't rocks ever say 'thank you'?
They take everything for granite.

A person bought a music stool and took it back the next day, complaining that it hadn't yet played a note.

CUSTOMER: Do you keep stationery?
SHOP ASSISTANT: No, I go home for lunch.

What did Neptune say when the sea dried up?
'I haven't a notion.'

'I've got a new pack of cards.'
'That's not such a big deal.'

BOSS: You understand the importance of punctuation in this job on the magazine, don't you?
SECRETARY: Oh, yes, I always get to work on time.

Did you hear about the band called Instant Potato?
They had a smash hit.

Why did Michael Jackson call his album *Bad*?
Because he couldn't spell 'Awful'.

What's pointed in one direction and headed in another?
A pin.

What has knobs on the front and wobbles?
Jellyvision.

OSCAR: Did you go to Oliver's party?
OTTO: No, the invitation said 'four to eight' and I'm nine.

What's the best way to keep water out of the house?
Don't pay your water rates.

What goes pedal, pedal, crash?
An idiot riding a bike.

Why couldn't the idiot open the piano?
All the keys were on the inside.

What's the difference betwen Chris Evans and the M25?
You can turn off the M25.

MATTIE: Can I go out and play?
MUM: What, with that filthy jumper?
MATTIE: No, with Jenny next door.

How do you become a professor?
By degrees.

What did Cinderella say when her photos didn't arrive?
'One day my prints will come.'

The first time he'd ever held up a shop a burglar went
into a pawnbroker's and said, 'Hands up or I shoot.'
'I'll give you £20 for the gun,' said the pawnbroker.

What do you call a popular perfume?
A best smeller.

What's round, white and smelly?
A ping-pong ball.

Why is perfume obedient?
Because it's scent wherever it goes.

What goes, 'Ha, ha, ha, clonk'?
A man laughing his head off.

What do you call small Indian guitars?
Baby sitars.

Why did the jockey take his saddle to bed?
In case he had nightmares.

What did Hamlet say when he found he was putting on weight?
'Tubby or not tubby, that is the question.'

What did Hamlet say when he had been watching too much TV?
'Teletubby, or not Teletubby, that is the question.'

What's another name for an adult?
Someone who's stopped growing except around the waist.

Why are adults boring?
Because they're groan-ups.

What's green, dangerous and grows in fields?
Grass.

But why is it dangerous?
It's full of blades.

Why did the authorities put a fence round the cemetery?
Because people were dying to get in.

What's black, floats on water and shouts, 'Knickers!'?
Crude oil.

What's black, floats on water and shouts, 'Underwear!'?
Refined oil.

What does a cat have that no other animal has?
Kittens.

What's the difference betwen a girl and a postage stamp?
One's a female; the other's a mail fee.

What's the difference between a tube and a crazy Dutchman?
One's a hollow cylinder; the other's a silly Hollander.

What's the difference between the Prince of Wales and a tennis ball?
One's heir to the throne; the other's thrown in the air.

TEACHER: What do we get from whales?
DENNIS: Coal, sir.
TEACHER: No, not the country, whales in the sea.
DENNIS: Sea-coal, sir.

Why did the loony stand on his head?
He was turning things over in his mind.

MUM: Did you learn anything new in school today?
NAUGHTY NIGEL: Yes, how to get out of maths by stuffing a hanky covered with red ink up my nose.

PETER: I think my mum's trying to tell me something.
ANITA: Why's that?
PETER: She keeps wrapping my sandwiches in a road map.

PASSENGER: Stop the bus! An old lady's just fallen off!
CONDUCTOR: That's all right, sir, she'd paid her fare.

Why did the old lady put wheels on her rocking-chair?
Because she wanted to rock and roll.

What colours should you paint the sun and the wind?
The sun rose and the wind blue.

Why is a river rich?
It has two banks.

When should you feed goat's milk to a baby?
When it's a baby goat.

Why do cows wear bells?
Their horns don't work.

What's white and goes up?
A silly snowflake.

What goes 99, plonk, 99, plonk, 99, plonk?
A centipede with a wooden leg.

What's yellow and very dangerous?
Shark-infested custard.

TEACHER: What does Hastings 1066 mean to you, Henry?
HENRY: William the Conqueror's phone number, sir?

Did you hear that they're going to open a tellycost in the High Street?
What's a tellycost?
About £100.

TEACHER: How can we stop food going bad?
SAMANTHA: Eat it.

TEACHER: Where is the River Rhine?
DONALD: You're the geography teacher, you tell me!

TEACHER: What does it mean when the barometer falls?
HETTIE: That the nail's come out of the wall.

TEACHER: It's time for your violin lesson.
PERCY: Oh, fiddle!

What do you get if there is a queue outide the barber's shop?
A barbercue.

Why did the idiot's bike have flat tyres?
So he could reach the pedals.

JOE: What did you get on your birthday?
FLO: A year older.

What can go up a chimney down but can't go down a chimney up?
An umbrella.

NURSE: May I take your pulse?
PATIENT: Haven't you got one of your own?

How can you lose 20 lbs at a stroke?
Cut your head off.

What vegetable plays snooker?
A cue-cumber.

What does a pig use to write a letter?
Pen and oink.

Did you hear about the stupid tap-dancer?
He fell in the sink.

What did one eye say to the other?
'Between us is something that smells.'

What runs around a field without moving?
A fence.

Why did the train say 'ouch' when it sat down?
It had a tender behind.

How can you keep from dying?
Stay in the living-room.

Why did the farmer plant razor blades next to his potatoes?
He wanted to grow chips.

CUSTOMER: Half a kilo of kiddles, please.
BUTCHER: You mean kidneys.
CUSTOMER: That's what I said, diddle I?

Why did the man sleep in his garage?
He didn't want to walk in his sleep.

STEVE: I'm glad I wasn't born in Germany.
STEPH: Why?
STEVE: I can't speak German.

SUNDAY SCHOOL TEACHER: Who sits on the right hand of God?
PUPIL: Er, Mrs God?

MUM: Harry, have you got your shoes on yet?
HARRY: Yes, Mum, all except one.

DAD: What did you learn in school today?
SIDNEY: That those sums you did for me were wrong!

'But Mummy, I don't want to go to Australia!"
'Shut up and keep digging!'

Young Dennis hadn't been to school for three days, and his mother didn't know where he was. His teacher asked her, 'Have you given the police a description of him?'
    'I tried,' said Dennis's mother, 'but they didn't believe me.'

How did the chimpanzee get out of his cage?
He used a monkey wrench.

Who was Erik the Red?
A Norse of a different colour.

What goes up and never comes down?
Your age.

What's guerilla warfare?
When monkeys throw nuts at each other.

What does 'climate' mean?
It's what you do with a ladder.

What's a fjord?
A Norwegian car.

What's an octopus?
A cat with eight legs.

What does millennium mean?
It's an insect with an awful lot of legs.

When do kettles have scale?
When they sing instead of whistle.

Who wrote *How to Pass Exams*?
Anne Sirs.

HOTEL GUEST: I'd like a room, please.
RECEPTIONIST: Single?
HOTEL GUEST: Yes, but I am engaged.

DEAN: I've just swallowed a bone.
JEAN: Are you choking?
DEAN: No, I'm serious.

Which composers do you find in a supermarket?
Chopin, Liszt.

Why is someone learning to sing like a person opening a tin of sardines?
They both have trouble with the key.

What never asks questions but gets a lot of answers?
The doorbell.

What kind of coat can you only put on when it's wet?
A coat of paint.

TOMMY: Dad, can I use the car?
DAD: What are your feet for?
TOMMY: One for the accelerator, one for the brake.

Why can't a car play football?
It only has one boot.

MRS BROWN: A man called to see you this afternoon.
MR BROWN: Did he have a bill?
MRS BROWN: No, just an ordinary nose.

What's the difference beween a bus driver and a cold?
One knows the stops; the other stops the nose.

BUS PASSENGER: Do you stop at the Grand Hotel?
BUS CONDUCTOR: Not on my salary!

'Mum, a black cat just walked into our kitchen.'
'That's all right, black cats are lucky.'
'This one wasn't, he's just eaten our supper.'

Why is a football stadium cool?
Because there's a fan in every seat.

How do you make a bandstand?
Take all their chairs away!

JIM: I've borrowed our neighbour's violin.
TIM: But you can't play it, can you?
JIM: No, but neither can he if I've got it!

How do you make antifreeze?
Hide her thermal underwear!

OPTICIAN: Have your eyes ever been checked?
PATIENT: No, they've always been this colour.

What do Eskimos sing at a birthday party?
'Freeze a jolly good fellow.'

Where do Eskimos like to dance?
At snowballs.

How can you make money fast?
Glue it to the table.

JAYNE: There's only one way to make money.
WAYNE: What's that?
JAYNE: I might have known you wouldn't know.

MUM: You've been fighting again! Didn't I tell you to count to ten before you lose your temper?
JOHNNY: Yes, Mum, but Jeff's mum only told him to count up to five and he hit me first.

What should you do with old fingernails?
File them.

Who invented fire?
Some bright spark.

What happens if you irritate a kangaroo?
It gets hopping mad.

Why do footballers wear shorts?
Because they'd be arrested if they didn't.

FIRST GARDENER: I used to work with hundreds under me.
SECOND GARDENER: Where was that?
FIRST GARDENER: I used to cut the grass in a cemetery.

OPTICIAN: You need glasses.
PATIENT: But I'm already wearing glasses.
OPTICIAN: Then I need glasses.

Why was the glow-worm upset?
Because she didn't know whether she was coming or glowing.

What do you feed young gnomes on?
Elf-raising flour.

Why did the man comb his hair with his toes?
To make both ends meet.

CUSTOMER: A reel of invisible thread, please.
SHOPKEEPER: Here you are, madam.
CUSTOMER: Thank you. You're sure it's invisible?
**SHOPKEEPER: Yes, madam. This is the third I've
sold this morning and we've been out of stock for
a week.**

What's the safest way to use a hammer?
Get someone else to hold the nails.

What's an inkling?
A baby fountain pen.

MRS GREEN: Does your husband have life insurance?
**MRS BROWN: No, just fire insurance. He says he
knows where he's going!**

AMY: How's your new boyfriend?
ANNIE: He's got an iron deficiency.
AMY: What do you mean?
ANNIE: His shirts always need ironing.

What is junk?
Something you keep for years and then throw away just before you need it.

JOHN: I like Christmas. All that kissing girls under the mistletoe.
DON: I prefer kissing them under the nose.

TENANT: When I left my last flat my landlord wept.
NEW LANDLORD: I shan't do that, I ask for rent in advance.

LECTURER: Would anyone like to ask a question?
MEMBER OF AUDIENCE: Yes, when are you going home?

What has 20 legs but can't walk?
Ten pairs of trousers.

How many letters are there in the alphabet?
Twenty-four.
Twenty-four?
Yes. ET went home.

How do you spell 'hungry horse' in four letters?
MTGG.

What's long-haired and has purple feet?
A lion that makes its own wine.

Why do lions eat raw meat?
Because no one ever teaches them how to cook.

How can you find a lost rabbit?
Make a noise like a carrot.

How does one magician greet another?
'How's tricks?'

Why do doctors and nurses wear masks?
So that if they make a mistake no one will know who it was.

What has three tails, 12 legs and can't see?
Three blind mice.

How did the Japanese businessman make so much money?
He had a yen for that kind of thing.

What did the dirt say to the rain?
'If you keep on, my name will be mud!'

'This coffee tastes like mud!'
'It was ground this morning.'

TEACHER: Who can tell me the name of a shooting star?
RYAN: Clint Eastwood.

What did the balloon say to the pin?
'Hi, buster!'

What do you call musical insects?
Humbugs.

PASSER-BY: And what's your name, little girl?
SUSIE: Susie.
PASSER-BY: And what's your surname?
SUSIE: I don't know. I'm not married yet.

POSTMAN: Is this letter for you? The name's smudged.
MR GREEN: Then it can't be. My name's Green.

What sits on the seabed and shivers?
A nervous wreck.

DUMBO: Why have you got tomatoes in your ears?
DIMBO: Could you speak up, please? I've got tomatoes in my ears.

JUDGE: Order! Order in court!
PRISONER: Egg and chips twice, please.

'Why are you paddling in your socks?'
'The water's cold at this time of year.'

ROMEO: You remind me of a pie.
JULIET: Because I'm all sweetness and light?
ROMEO: No, because you're crusty.

JERRY: What kind of dog is that?
TERRY: A police dog.
JERRY: It doesn't look much like a police dog.
TERRY: That's because it's a plain-clothes police dog.

JACK: Will you be my wife one day?
JILL: Not for one minute, creep!

What goes 'putt, putt, putt, putt'?
A poor golfer.

How do robots sit down?
Bolt upright.

CUSTOMER: When I bought this car you said it was rust-free. But look at its underneath! It's covered in rust!
SALESMAN: I sold you the car, sir, but the rust was free.

What kind of sandwich speaks for itself?
A tongue sandwich.

Why did the man have a sausage stuck behind his ear?
Because he'd eaten his pencil at lunch time.

HEAD TEACHER: I hear you missed school yesterday.
CUTHBERT: Not a bit!

WALLY: I hear your sister is the school swot.
SOLLY: Yes, she's killed more flies than anyone else in her class.

TRAVEL AGENT: Rooms overlooking the sea cost £10 a night extra.
HOLIDAYMAKER: What if I promise not to look?

TREV: How many seconds are there in a year?
KEV: I don't know.
TREV: Twelve.
KEV: Twelve?
TREV: Yes, 2nd January, 2nd February . . .

What animals do secret agents keep as pets?
Spy-ders.

Why did the secretary cut off the ends of her fingers?
So she could write shorthand.

JIMMY: Have you ever seen a man-eating shark?
TIMMY: No, but I've seen a man eating cod.

CUSTOMER: I'm looking for something cheap and nasty
to buy my mother-in-law for Christmas.
**SHOP ASSISTANT: I've got just the thing – my
father-in-law.**

How long does it take to learn how to skate?
About a dozen sittings.

What's the difference between a skunk and a rabbit?
The skunk uses a cheaper deodorant.

MUM: Why are you home from school early?
**DARREN: I was sent home because the boy who
sits next to me was smoking.**
MUM: But if he was smoking, why were you sent home?
DARREN: It was me that set him alight.

What did the fighting snails do?
Slugged it out.

KEN: Why do you put your hand to your mouth when
you sneeze?
LEN: To catch my teeth.

ZACH: Why are your socks inside out?
JACK: They've got holes on the other side.

TILLY: Will you join me in a cup of tea?
MILLY: Do you think there'd be room for both of us?

What do you call fake spaghetti?
Mockoroni.

How long should you cook spaghetti?
About 20 centimetres.

JULIE: How do you spell 'enrietta?
MUM: Do you mean Henrietta?
JULIE: No, I've written the H already.

How do you spell 'mousetrap' in just three letters?
C-a-t.

What illness do spies suffer from?
Codes in the nose.

When is a teacher like a bird of prey?
When he watches you like a hawk.

How can you travel around on the seabed?
By taxi-crab.

What ticks on the wall?
Ticky paper.

PASSENGER ON PLANE: Does this plane travel faster than sound?
AIR HOSTESS: No, madam.
PASSENGER ON PLANE: What a relief. I want to talk to my friend.

Why do people laugh up their sleeves?
Because that's where their funny bones are.

What do corn flakes wear on their feet?
K-logs

What's white, woolly and can see just as well from either end?
A sheep with its eyes closed.

What did the hat say to the head?
'I've got you covered.'

And finally . . .

Knock, knock.
Who's there?
Saul.
Saul who?
Saul over now!